.NET Interview Questions for Freshers and Experienced

ASP.NET,C#,MSSQL,MVC,WEB API

First Edition

Er. Vaibhav Singh Chauhan

Dedicating this book to the Universe within us.

वक्रतुण्ड महाकाय सूर्यकोटिसमप्रभ।
निर्विघ्नं कुरु मे देव सर्वकार्येषु सर्वदा॥

Contents

Preface

This book covers .NET Interview questions from almost every topic that is asked in an interview for a .NET Web Developer. Currently, it covers ASP.NET,C#, MSSQl,MVC, and Web API. I will try to furthermore in upcoming editions of this book.

This book has questions for both freshers and experienced candidates.I have added almost all questions that I have came across in my carrier. I have faced many interviews myself as a .NET Developer so I know the concerns of candidates and I have also taken many interviews which makes me familiar with the other side too.

Although I have tried to cover many questions and answered them in brief. You are advised to have further knowledge by digging deep in case you are not familiar with a concept as the explanation is short for many questions. For the few most important sorts of questions, I have given a long description that might help the candidate further. In case you find any typo or error in the book or if you want to contact me in case of any queries you can mail me directly at er_vaibhavsingh@yahoo.com

Overall point is that once you cover all questions mentioned in this book, probably more than 90% of interview questions on the given topics will be from this book.

All the best for your Interview Preparations

Er. Vaibhav Singh Chauhan

12th May 2021

About Author

Er. Vaibhav Singh Chauhan is a software consultant and has wide experience working in a corporate environment. He has served as Project Leader and Team Lead in some reputed organizations working for Swedish, US, UK, Japanese and Indian clients.

.NET Technolgy is the foundation of technology through which he started his carrier. So he has a sound knowledge of the platform and services used.

Website   : https://vaibonline.com

Email   : Er_VaibhavSingh@yahoo.com

General Questions

1. Introduce Yourself?

Freshers: I have pursued my Engineering from Lakshmi Narayan College of Technology, Bhopal which is a prestigious institute in central India. My specialization was Computer Science Engineering. I know to program with C# using OOPS concepts and some knowledge with MSSQL as Data Query Language. I have made my Major project using the same technology with the name
"Project name".

Experienced: I have a total experience of 8 years and an overall experience of 7 Years in .NET technology. Throughout my carrier, mostly I have used C# as a programming language using .NET Framework and MSSQL as RDBMS. I also got a chance to work with ASP.NET Webforms applications; MVC Razor-based applications, Web API, and WCF. I have also got experience with Desktop applications using Windows Form and WPF. I have experience with design patterns and Agile for Development. I also got the chance to work as a Team Lead/Tech lead in the last couple of organizations. Talking about the project domain/types, I have worked with E-gov organizations, E-commerce, product-based, Service-based, Heath Domain, Finance Domain projects.

Note: Customize a bit as per Job Description (JD).

2. Explain your Major Project/ Current Project for Experienced Candidates?

Explain the project architecture, team size, your role, and responsibilities in the project.

3. What is the reason for the job change?

You need to find the best reason as you already know it deep down. Some reasons can be
Late salary payment, Appraisal concerns, unhappiness with the technology you are currently working with, and such reasons.

4. What is the reason for the gap/Break-in Education/Experience?

You already know the real reason behind it. Explain the family situations or other reasons that occurred during that time. And at the end don't forget to mention that everything is well now and you are ready and very enthusiastic about this job.

5. Why so frequent switches?

In case you have switched organizations frequently, be prepared for this question. You need to give the best reasons to support your argument. There may be contractual jobs, explain them those contacts or there might be a company which has shut down its operation. So you need to write down a good reason on paper for every switch.

6.How will you rate yourself on a scale of 1-5 in C#

The interviewer may as this question before starting your technical interview. Be careful while rating yourself. Don't go for 5 unless you are a genius in that particular technology.

7.Where would you like to see yourself in the next 5 years?

Generally, the interviewer asks this question at the very end of the interview and mostly to freshers. By that time you will get a bit familiar with the interviewer and you will kind of know him/her. Get your answer accordingly. Generally, a Team Lead / Tech Lead is fine to say. You can also go for higher posts like a project manager or furthermore but be cautious in case your interviewer is too judge type.

8. Explain any one situation in which you did extraordinary in some project work?

Generally asked to experienced candidates. Be ready with a case where you have used some higher concepts and produced some good results which were very unusual. So better be a short storyteller for such questions. It's just a question to get an idea about you. Be confident and make some notes about it.

ASP.NET

1. What is ASP.Net?

It is a framework developed by Microsoft on which we can develop new generation web sites using web forms(aspx), MVC, HTML, Javascript, CSS etc. Its successor of Microsoft Active Server Pages(ASP). Currently there is ASP.NET 4.0, which is used to develop web sites. There are various page extensions provided by Microsoft that are being used for web site development. Eg: aspx, asmx, ascx, ashx, cs, vb, html, XML etc.

2. What are the advantages of ASP.NET?

ASP.Net is the next generation of ASP technology platform. It is superior to ASP in the following ways:

- Highly Scalable
- Compiled Code
- User Authentication
- Language Support
- Third party control
- Configuration and Deployment are easy.
- Object and Page caching
- Strict coding requirements

3. What's the use of Response.Output.Write()?

We can write formatted output using Response.Output.Write().

4. In which event of page cycle is the ViewState available?

After the Init() and before the Page_Load().

5. What is the difference between Server.Transfer and Response.Redirect?

In Server.Transfer page processing transfers from one page to the other page without making a round-trip back to the client's browser. This provides a faster response with a little less overhead on the server. The clients url history list or current url Server does not update in case of Server.Transfer.

Response.Redirect is used to redirect the user's browser to another page or site. It performs trip back to the client where the client's browser is redirected to the new page. The user's browser history list is updated to reflect the new address.

6. From which base class all Web Forms are inherited?

Page class.

7. What are the different validators in ASP.NET?

1. Required field Validator
2. Range Validator
3. Compare Validator
4. Custom Validator
5. Regular expression Validator
6. Summary Validator

8. Which validator control you use if you need to make sure the values in two different controls matched?

Compare Validator control.

9. What is the concept of Postback in ASP.NET?

Postback is a request which is sent from a client to the server from the same page user is working with. There is an HTTP POST request mechanism in ASP.NET. It posts a complete page back to the server to refresh the whole page.

10. What is the used of "isPostBack" property?

The "IsPostBack" property of page object is used to check that the page is posted back or not.

11. How do you identify that the page is PostBack?

There is a property named "IsPostBack" property in Post object, which can be checked to know that the page is posted back.

12. What is ViewState?

ViewState is used to retain the state of server-side objects between page post backs.

13. Where the viewstate is stored after the page postback?

ViewState is stored in a hidden field on the page at client side. ViewState is transported to the client and back to the server, and is not stored on the server or any other external source.

14. How long the items in ViewState exists?

They exist for the life of the current page.

15. What are the different Session state management options available in ASP.NET?

1. In-Process
2. Out-of-Process.

In-Process stores the session in memory on the web server.

Out-of-Process Session state management stores data in an external server. The external server may be either a SQL Server or a State Server. All objects stored in session are required to be serializable for Out-of-Process state management.

16. How you can add an event handler?

Using the Attributes property of server side control.

e.g.

```
btnSubmit.Attributes.Add("onMouseOver","JavascriptCode();")
```

17. What is caching?

Caching is a technique used to increase performance by keeping frequently accessed data or files in memory. The request for a cached file/data will be accessed from cache instead of actual location of that file.

18. what are the main requirements for caching?

- By caching the response, your request is served by the response already stored in memory.
- You must be very careful while choosing the items to cache because Caching incurs overhead.
- A frequently used web form which data doesn't frequently change is good for caching.
- A cached web form freezes form?s server-side content, and changes to that content do not appear until the cache is refreshed.

19. What are the different types of caching? ASP.NET has 3 kinds of caching :

1. Output Caching,
2. Fragment Caching,
3. Data Caching.

20. Which type if caching will be used if we want to cache the portion of a page instead of whole page?

Fragment Caching: It caches the portion of the page generated by the request. For that, we can create user controls with the below code:

```
<%@ OutputCache Duration="120" VaryByParam="CategoryID;SelectedID" %>
```

21. List the events in page life cycle.

1) Page_PreInit
2) Page_Init
3) Page_InitComplete
4) Page_PreLoad
5) Page_Load
6) Page_LoadComplete
7) Page_PreRender
8) Render

22. Can we have a web application running without web.Config file?

Yes

23. What is the difference between ASP.NET Webforms and ASP.NET MVC?

ASP.NET Webforms uses the *page controller* approach for rendering layout. In this approach, every page has its controller.

On the other hand, ASP.NET MVC uses the *Front Controller* approach. In this approach, there is a common controller for all pages.

24. Is it possible to create web application with both webforms and mvc?

Yes. We have to include below mvc assembly references in the web forms application to create hybrid application.

System.Web.Mvc

System.Web.Razor

System.ComponentModel.DataAnnotations

25. Can we add code files of different languages in App_Code folder?

No. The code files must be in same language to be kept in App_code folder.

26. What is Protected Configuration?

It is a feature used to secure connection string information.

27. Write code to send e-mail from an ASP.NET application?

```
MailMessage mailMess = new MailMessage ();
mailMess.From = "abc@gmail.com
        ";
mailMess.To = "xyz@gmail.com";
mailMess.Subject = "Test email";
mailMess.Body = "Hi This is a test mail.";
SmtpMail.SmtpServer = "localhost";
SmtpMail.Send (mailMess);
```

MailMessage and SmtpMail are classes defined System.Web.Mail namespace.

28. How can we prevent browser from caching an ASPX page?

We can SetNoStore on HttpCachePolicy object exposed by the Response object's Cache property:

```
Response.Cache.SetNoStore ();
Response.Write (DateTime.Now.ToLongTimeString ());
```

29. What is the good practice to implement validations in aspx page?

Client-side validation is the best way to validate data of a web page. It reduces the network traffic and saves server resources.

30. What is the use of Global.asax file?

The Global.asax file is used to execute the application-level events and sets application-level variables.

31. What is event bubbling?

When child control sends events to parent, it is termed as event bubbling. Server controls like Data Grid, Data List, and Repeater can have other child controls inside them.

32. What are the event handlers that we can have in Global.asax file?

Application Events: Application_Start , Application_End, Application_AcquireRequestState, Application_AuthenticateRequest, Application_AuthorizeRequest, Application_BeginRequest, Application_Disposed, Application_EndRequest, Application_Error, Application_PostRequestHandlerExecute, Application_PreRequestHandlerExecute,Application_PreSendRequestContent, Application_PreSendRequestHeaders, Application_ReleaseRequestState, Application_ResolveRequestCache, Application_UpdateRequestCache

Session Events: Session_Start,Session_End

33. Which *protocol is used to call a Web service*?

HTTP Protocol

34. Can we have multiple web config files for an asp.net application?

Yes.

35. What is the difference between web config and machine config?

Web config file is specific to a web application where as machine config is specific to a machine or server. There can be multiple web config files into an application where as we can have only one machine config file on a server.

36. Explain role based security ?

Role-based security is used in almost all organization, and the Role-based security assigns certain privileges to each role.

- o Each user is assigned a particular role from the list.
- o Privileges as per role restrict the user's actions on the system and ensure that a user can do only what he is permitted to do on the system.

```
<AUTHORIZATION>< authorization >

< allow roles="Domain_Name\Administrators" / >   < !-- Allow Administrators in domain. -- >

< deny users="*" / >                  < !-- Deny anyone else. -- >

< /authorization >
```

37. What is Cross Page Posting?

When we click submit button on a web page, the page post the data to the same page. The technique in which we post the data to different pages is called Cross Page posting. This can be achieved by setting POSTBACKURL property of the button that causes the postback. Findcontrol method of PreviousPage can be used to get the posted values on the page to which the page has been posted.

38. How can we apply Themes to an asp.net application?

We can specify the theme in web.config file. Below is the code example to apply theme:

```
<configuration>


<system.web>


<pages theme="Windows7" />


</system.web>
```

</configuration>

39. What is RedirectPermanent in ASP.Net?

RedirectPermanent Performs a permanent redirection from the requested URL to the specified URL. Once the redirection is done, it also returns 301 Moved Permanently responses.

40. What is MVC?

MVC is a framework used to create web applications. The web application base builds on Model-View-Controller pattern which separates the application logic from UI, and the input and events from the user will be controlled by the Controller.

41. Explain the working of passport authentication.

First of all it checks passport authentication cookie. If the cookie is not available then the application redirects the user to Passport Sign on page. Passport service authenticates the user details on sign on page and if valid then stores the authenticated cookie on client machine and then redirect the user to requested page

42. What are the advantages of Passport authentication?

All the websites can be accessed using single login credentials. So no need to remember login credentials for each web site.

Users can maintain his/ her information in a single location.

43. What are the asp.net Security Controls?

- <asp:Login>: Provides a standard login capability that allows the users to enter their credentials
- <asp:LoginName>: Allows you to display the name of the logged-in user
- <asp:LoginStatus>: Displays whether the user is authenticated or not
- <asp:LoginView>: Provides various login views depending on the selected template
- <asp:PasswordRecovery>: email the users their lost password

44. How do you register JavaScript for webcontrols ? We can register javascript for controls using <CONTROL - name>Attribtues.Add(scriptname,scripttext) method.

45. In which event are the controls fully loaded?

Page load event.

46. what is boxing and unboxing?

Boxing is assigning a value type to reference type variable.

Unboxing is reverse of boxing ie. Assigning reference type variable to value type variable.

47. Differentiate strong typing and weak typing

In strong typing, the data types of variable are checked at compile time. On the other hand, in case of weak typing the variable data types are checked at runtime. In case of strong typing, there is no chance of compilation error. Scripts use weak typing and hence issues arises at runtime.

48. How we can force all the validation controls to run?

The Page.Validate() method is used to force all the validation controls to run and to perform validation.

49. List all templates of the Repeater control.

- ItemTemplate
- AlternatingItemTemplate
- SeparatorTemplate
- HeaderTemplate
- FooterTemplate

50. List the major built-in objects in ASP.NET?

- Application
- Request

- Response
- Server
- Session
- Context
- Trace

51. What is the appSettings Section in the web.config file?

The appSettings block in web config file sets the user-defined values for the whole application.

For example, in the following code snippet, the specified ConnectionString section is used throughout the project for database connection:

```
<em><configuration>

<appSettings>

<add key="ConnectionString" value="server=local; pwd=password; database=default" />

</appSettings></em>
```

52. Which data type does the RangeValidator control support?

The data types supported by the RangeValidator control are Integer, Double, String, Currency, and Date.

53. What is the difference between an HtmlInputCheckBox control and an HtmlInputRadioButton control?

In HtmlInputCheckBoxcontrol, multiple item selection is possible whereas in HtmlInputRadioButton controls, we can select only single item from the group of items.

54. Which namespaces are necessary to create a localized application?

System.Globalization

System.Resources

55. What is a cookie?

A Cookie is a small piece of information which is stored at the client side. There are two types of cookie:

- o Session/Temporary Cookie: valid for a single session
- o Persistent Cookie: valid for multiple session

56. What is the default timeout for a cookie?

30 minutes.

57. How would you turn off cookies on a page of a website?

You have to follow the procedures given below:

- o Use the "Cookie.Discard" property.
- o It gets or sets the discard flag set by the server.
- o When set to true, this property instructs the client application not to save the Cookie on the hard disk of the user at the end of the session.

58. What are the different types of cookies in ASP.NET?

Session Cookie – Resides on the client machine for a single session until the user does not log out.

Persistent Cookie – Resides on a user's machine for a period specified for its expiry, such as 10 days, one month, and never.

59. What is the file extension of web service?

Web services have file extension .asmx..

60. What are the components of ADO.NET?

The components of ADO.Net are Dataset, Data Reader, Data Adaptor, Command, connection.

61. What is the difference between ExecuteScalar and ExecuteNonQuery?

ExecuteScalar returns output value where as ExecuteNonQuery does not return any value but the number of rows affected by the query. ExecuteScalar used for fetching a single value and ExecuteNonQuery used to execute Insert and Update statements.

62. What is IIS?

IIS stands for Internet Information Services. It is created by Microsoft to provide Internet-based services to ASP.NET Web applications.

63. What is the usage of IIS?

Following are the main usage of IIS:

- IIS is used to make your computer to work as a Web server and provides the functionality to develop and deploy Web applications on the server.
- IIS handles the request and response cycle on the Web server.
- IIS also offers the services of SMTP and FrontPage server extensions.
- The SMTP is used to send emails and use FrontPage server extensions to get the dynamic features of IIS, such as form handler.

64. What is a multilingual website?

If a website provides content in many languages, it is known as a multilingual website. It contains multiple copies of its content and other resources, such as date and time, in different languages.

65. What is the parent class of all web server control?

System.Web.UI.Control class

66. What is the difference between the GET method () and POST method ()?

GetMethod

Data is affixed to the URL.

Data is not secured.

Data transmission is faster in this method.

It is a single call system.

Only a limited amount of data can be sent.

It is a default method for many browsers.

PostMethod

Data is not affixed to the URL

Data is secured.

Data transmission is comparatively slow

It is a two call system

A large amount of data can be sent

It is not set as default. It should be explicitly specified

67. What is the difference between session object and application object?

The session object is used to maintain the session of each user. A session id is generated if a user enters in the application and when the user leaves the application, the session id is automatically deleted.

On the other hand, the application object is used to store the information and access variables from any page in the application.

68. What is the difference between trace and debug?

Debug class is used to debug builds. Trace class is used for both debug and release builds.

69. What is the difference between client-side and server-side validations in WebPages?

The client-side validation happens at the client's side with the help of JavaScript and VBScript. This validation has occurred before the Web page is sent to the server.

The server-side validation happens at the server side.

70. What is the difference between file-based dependency and key-based dependency?

File-based dependency: File-based dependency facilitates you to save the dependency on a file in a disk.

Key-based dependency: In key-based dependency, you depend on another cached item.

71. What is the difference between globalization and localization?

Globalization: Globalization is a technique to identify the part of a Web application that is different for different languages and separate it out from the web application.

Localization: In localization, you try to configure a Web application so that it can be supported for a specific language or locale.

72. What is the difference between a page theme and a global theme?

Page Theme: The page theme is applied to particular web pages of the project. It is stored inside a subfolder of the App_Themes folder.

Global Theme: The Global theme is applied to all the web applications on the web server. It is stored inside the Themes folder on a Web server.

73. What is the difference between early binding and late binding?

Early Binding: In early binding, a non-virtual method is called which is decided at a compile time.

Late Binding: In late binding, a virtual method is called which is decided at runtime.

74. What is the difference between server-side scripting and client-side scripting?

Server-side scripting: In server-side scripting, all the script are executed by the server and interpreted as needed.

Client-side scripting: In client-side scripting, the script will be executed immediately in the browser such as form field validation, email validation, etc.

The client-side scripting is usually carried out in VBScript or JavaScript.

75. How to sign out from forms authentication?

FormsAuthentication.Signout() method is used to sign out from forms authentication.

76. How to display validation messages in one control?

By the help of *ValidationSummary* control, we can display all validation messages in one control.

77. What is the difference between authentication and authorization?

Authentication is a process of identifying user whereas authorization is used to check the access rights of an identified user.

78. Which object encapsulates state or data of a user?

Session object.

79. What are the differences between the Response.Write() and Response.Output.Write()?

Response.Write() is used for normal output whereas *Response.Output.Write()* is used for formatted output.

80. Define the types of configuration files.

There are two types of configuration files:

- Application Level config = Web.config.
- Machine Level config = Machine.config.

81. What is the difference between Web config and Machine config files?

Web config file is specific to web application whereas Machine config file is specific to machine or server.

There can be multiple web config files in an application but only one machine config file.

82. What are the HTML server controls in ASP.NET?

- HTML server controls are just like HTML elements that we use on the HTML pages.
- HTML server controls are used to expose properties and events for use.
- To make these controls programmatically accessible, we specify that the HTML controls act as a server control by adding the runat="server" attribute.

C# Beginer To intermediate

1. What is C#?

C# is an object-oriented, type-safe, and managed language that is compiled by .Net framework to generate Microsoft Intermediate Language.

2. Explain types of comment in C# with examples

Single line

Example:

//This is a single line comment

ii. Multiple line (/* */)

Example:

/*This is a multiple line comment

We are in line 2

Last line of comment*/

iii. XML Comments (///).

Eg:

/// summary;

/// Set error message for multilingual language.

/// summary

3. Can multiple catch blocks be executed?

No, Multiple catch blocks can't be executed. Once the proper catch code executed, the control is transferred to the finally block, and then the code that follows the finally block gets executed.

4. What is the difference between public, static, and void?

Public declared variables or methods are accessible anywhere in the application. Static declared variables or methods are globally accessible without creating an instance of the class. Static member are by default not globally accessible it depends upon the type of access modified used. The compiler stores the address of the method as the entry point and uses this information to begin execution before any objects are created. And Void is a type modifier that states that the method or variable does not return any value.

5. What is an object?

An object is an instance of a class through which we access the methods of that class. "New" keyword is used to create an object. A class that creates an object in memory will contain the information about the methods, variables, and behavior of that class.

6. What is a Class?

A Class is an encapsulation of properties and methods that are used to represent a real-time entity. It is a data structure that brings all the instances together in a single unit.

7. Define Constructors

A constructor is a member function in a class that has the same name as its class. The constructor is automatically invoked whenever an object class is created. It constructs the values of data members while initializing the class.

8. What is the difference between ref & out parameters?

An argument passed as ref must be initialized before passing to the method whereas out parameter needs not to be initialized before passing to a method.

9. What is the use of 'using' statement in C#?

The 'using' block is used to obtain a resource and process it and then automatically dispose of when the execution of the block completed.

10. Can we use "this" command within a static method?

We can't use 'This' in a static method because we can only use static variables/methods in a static method.

11. What is the difference between constants and read-only?

Constant variables are declared and initialized at compile time. The value can't be changed afterward. Read-only is used only when we want to assign the value at run time.

12. What is an interface class? Give one example of it

An Interface is an abstract class which has only public abstract methods, and the methods only have the declaration and not the definition. These abstract methods must be implemented in the inherited classes.

```
using System;

using System.Collections.Generic;

using System.Linq;

using System.Text;

using System.Threading.Tasks;

namespace DemoApplication

{

interface Guru99Interface

{

void SetTutorial(int pID, string pName);

String GetTutorial();

}
```

```csharp
class Guru99Tutorial : Guru99Interface
{
protected int TutorialID;
protected string TutorialName;

public void SetTutorial(int pID, string pName)
{
 TutorialID = pID;
 TutorialName = pName;
}

public String GetTutorial()
{
 return TutorialName;
}

static void Main(string[] args)
{
 Guru99Tutorial pTutor = new Guru99Tutorial();

 pTutor.SetTutorial(1,".Net by Guru99");

 Console.WriteLine(pTutor.GetTutorial());
```

```
Console.ReadKey();
 }
}
}
```

13.The basis of comparison Between C# Interface vs Abstract Class

C# Interface

Access Specifier : In C#, Interface cannot have access specifier for functions. It is public by default.

Implementation : In C#, an interface can only have a signature, not the implementation.

Speed : Interface is comparatively slow.

Instantiate : Interface is absolutely abstract and cannot be instantiated.

Fields : Interface cannot have fields.

Methods: Methods

C# Abstract Class

Access Specifier : In C#, an abstract class can have access specifier for functions.

Implementation : An abstract class can provide complete implementation.

Speed: An abstract class is fast.

Instantiate: An abstract class cannot be instantiated.

Fields: An abstract class can have defined fields and constants

Methods: An abstract class can have non-abstract methods.

Basic Difference: Interfaces have all the methods having only declaration but no definition. In an abstract class, we can have some concrete methods. In an interface class, all the methods are public. An abstract class may have private methods.

14. What are value types and reference types?

A value type holds a data value within its own memory space. Example

```
int a = 30;
```

Reference type stores the address of the Object where the value is being stored. It is a pointer to another memory location.

```
string b = "Hello Guru99!!";
```

15. What are Custom Control and User Control?

Custom Controls are controls generated as compiled code (Dlls), those are easier to use and can be added to toolbox. Developers can drag and drop controls to their web forms. Attributes can, at design time. We can easily add custom controls to Multiple Applications (If Shared Dlls). So, If they are private, then we can copy to dll to bin directory of web application and then add reference and can use them.

User Controls are very much similar to ASP include files, and are easy to create. User controls can't be placed in the toolbox and dragged - dropped from it. They have their design and code-behind. The file extension for user controls is ascx.

16. What are sealed classes in C#?

We create sealed classes when we want to restrict the class to be inherited. Sealed modifier used to prevent derivation from a class. If we forcefully specify a sealed class as base class, then a compile-time error occurs.

17. What is method overloading?

Method overloading is creating multiple methods with the same name with unique signatures in the same class. When we compile, the compiler uses overload resolution to determine the specific method to be invoke.

18. What is an Array? Give the syntax for a single and multi-dimensional array?

An Array is used to store multiple variables of the same type. It is a collection of variables stored in a contiguous memory location.

For Example:

double numbers = new double[10];

int[] score = new int[4] {25,24,23,25};

A Single dimensional array is a linear array where the variables are stored in a single row. Above **example** is a Single dimensional array.

Arrays can have more than one dimension. Multidimensional arrays are also called rectangular arrays.

For Example, int[,] numbers = new int[3,2] { {1,2} ,{2,3},{3,4} };

19. Name some properties of Array.

Properties of an Array include:

- **Length** – Gets the total number of elements in an array.
- **IsFixedSize** – Tells whether the array is fixed in size or not.
- **IsReadOnly** – Tells whether the array is read-only or not.

20. What is an Array Class?

An **Array class** is the base class for all arrays. It provides many properties and methods. It is present in the namespace System.

21. What is the difference between Array and Arraylist?

In an array, we can have items of the same type only. The size of the array is fixed when compared. To an arraylist is similar to an array, but it doesn't have a fixed size.

22. What is Jagged Arrays?

The Array which has elements of type array is called jagged Array. The elements can be of different dimensions and sizes. We can also call jagged Array as an Array of arrays.

23. Can a private virtual method can be overridden?

No, because they are not accessible outside the class.

24. Describe the accessibility modifier "protected internal".

Protected Internal variables/methods are accessible within the same assembly and also from the classes that are derived from this parent class.

25. What are the differences between System.String and System.Text.StringBuilder classes?

System.String is immutable. When we modify the value of a string variable, then a new memory is allocated to the new value and the previous memory allocation released. System.StringBuilder was designed to have a concept of a mutable string where a variety of operations can be performed without allocation separate memory location for the modified string.

26. What's the difference between the System.Array.CopyTo() and System.Array.Clone() ?

Using Clone() method, we creates a new array object containing all the elements in the original Array and using CopyTo() method. All the elements of existing array copies into another existing array. Both methods perform a shallow copy.

27. How can we sort the elements of the Array in descending order?

Using Sort() methods followed by Reverse() method.

28. Write down the C# syntax to catch an exception

To catch an exception, we use try-catch blocks. Catch block can have a parameter of system.Exception type.

Eg:

```
try {
    GetAllData();
}
catch (Exception ex) {
}
```

In the above example, we can omit the parameter from catch statement.

29. What is the difference between Finalize() and Dispose() methods?

Dispose() is called when we want for an object to release any unmanaged resources with them. On the other hand, Finalize() is used for the same purpose, but it doesn't assure the garbage collection of an object.

Dispose

It is used to free unmanaged resources at any time.

It is called by user code and the class which is implementing dispose method, must has to implement IDisposable interface.

It is implemented by implementing IDisposable interface Dispose() method.

There is no performance costs associated with Dispose method.

Finalize

It can be used to free unmanaged resources held by an object before that object is destroyed.

It is called by Garbage Collector and cannot be called by user code.

It is implemented with the help of Destructors

There is performance costs associated with Finalize method since it doesn't clean the memory immediately and called by GC automatically.

30. What are circular references?

Circular reference is situation in which two or more resources are interdependent on each other causes the lock condition and make the resources unusable.

31. What are generics in C#.NET?

Generics are used to make reusable code classes to decrease the code redundancy, increase type safety, and performance. Using generics, we can create collection classes. To create generic collection, System.Collections.Generic namespace should be used instead of classes such as ArrayList in the System.Collections namespace. Generics promotes the usage of parameterized types.

32. What is an object pool in .NET?

An object pool is a container having objects ready to be used. It tracks the object that is currently in use, total number of objects in the pool. This reduces the overhead of creating and re-creating objects.

33. List down the commonly used types of exceptions in .net

ArgumentException, ArgumentNullException , ArgumentOutOfRangeException, ArithmeticException, DivideByZeroException ,OverflowException , IndexOutOfRangeException ,InvalidCastException ,InvalidOperationException , IOEndOfStreamException

, NullReferenceException , OutOfMemoryException , StackOverflowException etc.

34. What are Custom Exceptions?

Sometimes there are some errors that need to be handled as per user requirements. Custom exceptions are used for them and are used defined exceptions.

.

35. What is a Delegate? Explain.

A **Delegate** is a variable that holds the reference to a method. Hence it is a function pointer of reference type. All Delegates are derived from System.Delegate namespace. Both Delegate and the method that it refers to can have the same signature.

Declaring a delegate: *public delegate void AddNumbers(int n);*

After the declaration of a delegate, the object must be created of the delegate using the new keyword.

AddNumbers an1 = new AddNumbers(number);

The delegate provides a kind of encapsulation to the reference method, which will internally get called when a delegate is called.

1 public delegate int myDel(int number);

2 public class Program

3 {

4 public int AddNumbers(int a)

5 {

6 int Sum = a + 10;

7 return Sum;

8 }

9   public void Start()

10 {

11 myDel DelgateExample = AddNumbers;

12 }

13 }

In the above example, we have a delegate myDel which takes an integer value as a parameter. Class Program has a method of the same signature as the delegate, called AddNumbers().

If there is another method called Start() which creates an object of the delegate, then the object can be assigned to AddNumbers as it has the same signature as that of the delegate.

36. What are Events?

Events are user actions that generate notifications to the application to which it must respond. The user actions can be mouse movements, keypress and so on.

Programmatically, a class that raises an event is called a publisher and a class which responds/receives the event is called a subscriber. An Event should have at least one subscriber else that event is never raised.

Delegates are used to declare Events.

Public delegate void PrintNumbers();

Event PrintNumbers myEvent;

37. How to use Delegates with Events?

Delegates are used to raise events and handle them. Always a delegate needs to be declared first and then the Events are declared.

Let us see an Example:

Consider a class called Patient. Consider two other classes, Insurance, and Bank which requires Death information of the Patient from patient class. Here, Insurance and Bank are the subscribers and the Patient class becomes the Publisher. It triggers the death event and the other two classes should receive the event.

```
1 namespace ConsoleApp2

2 {

3 public class Patient

4 {

5 public delegate void deathInfo();//Declaring a Delegate//

6 public event deathInfo deathDate;//Declaring the event//

7 public void Death()

8 {

9   deathDate();

10 }

11 }

12 public class Insurance

13 {

14 Patient myPat = new Patient();

15 void GetDeathDetails()

16 {

17 //-------Do Something with the deathDate event-----------//
```

```
18 }

19 void Main()

20 {

21 //--------Subscribe the function GetDeathDetails----------//

22 myPat.deathDate += GetDeathDetails;

23 }

24 }

25 public class Bank

26 {

27 Patient myPat = new Patient();

28 void GetPatInfo ()

29 {

30 //-------Do Something with the deathDate event------------//

31 }

32 void Main()

33 {

34 //--------Subscribe the function GetPatInfo ----------//

35 myPat.deathDate += GetPatInfo;

36 }

37 }

38 }
```

38. What are the different types of Delegates?

The Different types of Delegates are:

Single Delegate – A delegate which can call a single method.

Multicast Delegate – A delegate which can call multiple methods. + and − operators are used to subscribe and unsubscribe respectively.

Generic Delegate – It does not require an instance of delegate to be defined. It is of three types, Action, Funcs and Predicate.

- *Action*– In the above example of delegates and events, we can replace the definition of delegate and event using Action keyword. The Action delegate defines a method that can be called on arguments but does not return a result

Public delegate void deathInfo();

Public event deathInfo deathDate;

//Replacing with Action//

Public event Action deathDate;

Action implicitly refers to a delegate.

- *Func* – A Func delegate defines a method that can be called on arguments and returns a result.
Func <int, string, bool> myDel is same as *delegate bool myDel(int a, string b);*

- *Predicate* – Defines a method that can be called on arguments and always returns the bool.
Predicate<string> myDel is same as *delegate bool myDel(string s);*

39. What's a multicast delegate?

A delegate having multiple handlers assigned to it is called multicast delegate. Each handler is assigned to a method. In other words

A Delegate that points to more than one method is called a Multicast Delegate. Multicasting is achieved by using + and += operator.

Consider the Example from previous delegate question

There are two subscribers for *deathEvent*, *GetPatInfo*, and *GetDeathDetails*. And hence we have used += operator. It means whenever the *myDel* is called, both the subscribers get called. The delegates will be called in the order in which they are added.

40. Explain Publishers and Subscribers in Events.

A Publisher is a class responsible for publishing a message of different types of other classes. The message is nothing but Event as discussed in the above questions.

From the **Example** in Question 32, Class Patient is the Publisher class. It is generating an Event *deathEvent*, which the other classes receive.

Subscribers capture the message of the type that it is interested in. Again, from the **Example** of Question 32, Class Insurance and Bank are Subscribers. They are interested in event *deathEvent* of type *void*.

41. How do you inherit a class into other class in C#?

Colon is used as inheritance operator in C#. Just place a colon and then the class name.

public class DerivedClass : BaseClass

42. What is the base class in .net from which all the classes are derived from?

System.Object

43. What is the difference between method overriding and method overloading?

In method overriding, we change the method definition in the derived class that changes the method behavior. Method overloading is creating a method with the same name within the same class having different signatures.

44. What are the different ways a method can be overloaded?

Methods can be overloaded using different data types for a parameter, different order of parameters, and different number of parameters.

45. Why can't you specify the accessibility modifier for methods inside the interface?

In an interface, we have virtual methods that do not have method definition. All the methods are there to be overridden in the derived class. That's why they all are public.

46. How can we set the class to be inherited, but prevent the method from being over-ridden?

Declare the class as public and make the method sealed to prevent it from being overridden.

47. What happens if the inherited interfaces have conflicting method names?

Implement is up to you as the method is inside your own class. There might be a problem when the methods from different interfaces expect different data, but as far as compiler cares you're okay.

48. What is the difference between a Struct and a Class?

Structs are value-type variables, and classes are reference types. Structs stored on the Stack causes additional overhead but faster retrieval. Structs cannot be inherited.

Class

Supports Inheritance

Class is Pass by reference (reference type)

Members are private by default

Good for larger complex objects

Can use waste collector for memory management

Struct

Does not support Inheritance

Struct is Pass by Copy (Value type)

Members are public by default

Good for Small isolated models

Cannot use Garbage collector and hence no Memory management

49. How to use nullable types in .Net?

Value types can take either their normal values or a null value. Such types are called nullable types.

```
Int? someID = null;
If(someID.HasVAlue)
{

}
```

50. How we can create an array with non-default values?

We can create an array with non-default values using Enumerable.Repeat.

51. What is difference between "is" and "as" operators in c#?

"is" operator is used to check the compatibility of an object with a given type, and it returns the result as Boolean.

"as" operator is used for casting of an object to a type or a class.

52. What are indexers in C# .NET?

Indexers are known as smart arrays in C#. It allows the instances of a class to be indexed in the same way as an array.

Eg:

```
public int this[int index]   // Indexer declaration
```

53. What is difference between the "throw" and "throw ex" in .NET?

"Throw" statement preserves original error stack whereas "throw ex" have the stack trace from their throw point. It is always advised to use "throw" because it provides more accurate error information.

54. What are C# attributes and its significance?

C# provides developers a way to define declarative tags on certain entities, eg. Class, method, etc. are called attributes. The attribute's information can be retrieved at runtime using Reflection.

55. How to implement a singleton design pattern in C#?

In a singleton pattern, a class can only have one instance and provides an access point to it globally.

Eg:

```
Public sealed class Singleton
{
Private static readonly Singleton _instance = new Singleton();
}
```

56. What is the difference between directcast and ctype?

DirectCast is used to convert the type of object that requires the run-time type to be the same as the specified type in DirectCast.

Ctype is used for conversion where the conversion is defined between the expression and the type.

57. What is Managed and Unmanaged code?

Ans: Managed code is a code which is executed by CLR (Common Language Runtime) i.e all application code based on .Net Platform. It is considered as managed because of the .Net framework which internally uses the garbage collector to clear up the unused memory.

Unmanaged code is any code that is executed by application runtime of any other framework apart from .Net. The application runtime will take care of memory, security and other performance operations.

58. Is C# code is managed or unmanaged code?

C# is managed code because Common language runtime can compile C# code to Intermediate language.

59. What is Console application?

A console application is an application that can be run in the command prompt in Windows. For any beginner on .Net, building a console application is ideally the first step, to begin with.

60. Give an example of removing an element from the queue

The dequeue method is used to remove an element from the queue.

```
using System;
using System.Collections;
```

```csharp
using System.Collections.Generic;

using System.Linq;

using System.Text;

using System.Threading.Tasks;


namespace DemoApplication

{

class Program

{

static void Main(string[] args)

{

Queue qt = new Queue();

qt.Enqueue(1);

qt.Enqueue(2);

qt.Enqueue(3);


foreach (Object obj in qt)

{

Console.WriteLine(obj);

}

Console.WriteLine(); Console.WriteLine();

Console.WriteLine("The number of elements in the Queue " + qt.Count);

Console.WriteLine("Does the Queue contain " + qt.Contains(3));

Console.ReadKey();

}
```

```
}

}
```

61. What are the fundamental OOP concepts?

The four fundamental concepts of Object Oriented Programming are:

- **Encapsulation** – The Internal representation of an object is hidden from the view outside object's definition. Only the required information can be accessed whereas the rest of the data implementation is hidden.
- **Abstraction** – It is a process of identifying the critical behavior and data of an object and eliminating the irrelevant details.
- **Inheritance** – It is the ability to create new classes from another class. It is done by accessing, modifying and extending the behavior of objects in the parent class.
- **Polymorphism** – The name means, one name, many forms. It is achieved by having multiple methods with the same name but different implementations.

62. What are the different types of classes in C#?

The different types of class in C# are:

- **Partial class** – Allows its members to be divided or shared with multiple .cs files. It is denoted by the keyword *Partial.*
- **Sealed class** – It is a class which cannot be inherited. To access the members of a sealed class, we need to create the object of the class. It is denoted by the keyword *Sealed.*
- **Abstract class** – It is a class whose object cannot be instantiated. The class can only be inherited. It should contain at least one method. It is denoted by the keyword *abstract.*
- **Static class** – It is a class which does not allow inheritance. The members of the class are also static. It is denoted by the keyword *static.* This keyword tells the compiler to check for any accidental instances of the static class.

63. Explain Code compilation in C#.

There are four steps in code compilation which include:

- Compiling the source code into Managed code by C# compiler.
- Combining the newly created code into assemblies.

- Loading the Common Language Runtime(CLR).
- Executing the assembly by CLR.

64. What is the difference between Virtual method and Abstract method?

A **Virtual method** must always have a default implementation. However, it can be overridden in the derived class, though not mandatory. It can be overridden using *override* keyword.

An **Abstract method** does not have an implementation. It resides in the abstract class. It is mandatory that the derived class implements the abstract method. An *override* keyword is not necessary here though it can be used.

65. Explain Namespaces in C#.

They are used to organize large code projects. "System" is the most widely used namespace in C#. We can create our own namespace and use one namespace in another, which are called Nested Namespaces.

They are denoted by the keyword "namespace".

66. Explain Abstraction.

Abstraction is one of the OOP concepts. It is used to display only the essential features of the class and hides the unnecessary information.

Let us take an Example of a Car:

A driver of the car should know the details about the Car such as color, name, mirror, steering, gear, brake, etc. What he doesn't have to know is an Internal engine, Exhaust system.

So, Abstraction helps in knowing what is necessary and hiding the internal details from the outside world. Hiding of the internal information can be achieved by declaring such parameters as Private using *the private* keyword.

67. Explain Polymorphism?

Programmatically, **Polymorphism** means same method but different implementations.

It is of 2 types, Compile-time and Runtime.

Compile time polymorphism is achieved by operator overloading.

Runtime polymorphism is achieved by overriding. Inheritance and Virtual functions are used during Runtime Polymorphism.

For Example, If a class has a method Void Add(), polymorphism is achieved by Overloading the method, that is, void Add(int a, int b), void Add(int add) are all overloaded methods.

68. What are C# I/O Classes? What are the commonly used I/O Classes?

C# has System.IO namespace, consisting of classes that are used to perform various operations on files like creating, deleting, opening, closing etc.

Some commonly used I/O classes are:

- **File** – Helps in manipulating a file.
- **StreamWriter** – Used for writing characters to a stream.
- **StreamReader** – Used for reading characters to a stream.
- **StringWriter** – Used for reading a string buffer.
- **StringReader** – Used for writing a string buffer.
- **Path** – Used for performing operations related to path information.

69. What is StreamReader/StreamWriter class?

StreamReader and StreamWriter are classes of namespace System.IO. They are used when we want to read or write charact90, Reader-based data, respectively.

Some of the members of StreamReader are: Close(), Read(), Readline().

Members of StreamWriter are: Close(), Write(), Writeline().

1 Class Program1

2 {

3 using(StreamReader sr = new StreamReader("C:\ReadMe.txt")

4 {

5 //----------------code to read------------------//

```
6 }
7 using(StreamWriter sw = new StreamWriter("C:\ReadMe.txt"))
8 {
9   //-------------code to write--------------------//
10 }
11 }
```

70. What is a Destructor in C#?

A **Destructor** is used to clean up the memory and free the resources. But in C# this is done by the garbage collector on its own. System.GC.Collect() is called internally for cleaning up. But sometimes it may be necessary to implement destructors manually.

For Example:

```
~Car()

{

Console.writeline("....");

}
```

71. What are Boxing and Unboxing?

Converting a value type to reference type is called **Boxing**.

For Example:

```
int Value1 -= 10;

//————Boxing——————//

object boxedValue = Value1;
```

Explicit conversion of same reference type (created by boxing) back to value type is called **Unboxing**.

For Example:

//—————UnBoxing——————//

int UnBoxing = int (boxedValue);

72. What is the difference between Continue and Break Statement?

Break statement breaks the loop. It makes the control of the program to exit the loop. **Continue statement** makes the control of the program to exit only the current iteration. It does not break the loop.

73. What is the difference between finally and finalize block?

finally **block** is called after the execution of try and catch block. It is used for exception handling. Regardless of whether an exception is caught or not, this block of code will be executed. Usually, this block will have clean-up code.

finalize method is called just before garbage collection. It is used to perform clean up operations of Unmanaged code. It is automatically called when a given instance is not subsequently called.

74. What is a String? What are the properties of a String Class?

A **String** is a collection of char objects. We can also declare string variables in c#.

string name = "C# Questions";

A string class in C# represents a string.

The properties of String class are **Chars and Length.**
Chars get the Char object in the current String.
Length gets the number of objects in the current String.

75.What is an Escape Sequence? Name some String escape sequences in C#.

An **Escape sequence** is denoted by a backslash (\). The backslash indicates that the character that follows it should be interpreted literally or it is a special character. An escape sequence is considered as a single character.

String escape sequences are as follows:

\n – Newline character
\b – Backspace
\\ – Backslash
\' – Single quote
\" – Double Quote

76. What are Regular expressions? Search a string using regular expressions?

Ans: Regular expression is a template to match a set of input. The pattern can consist of operators, constructs or character literals. Regex is used for string parsing and replacing the character string.

For Example:

* matches the preceding character zero or more times. So, a*b regex is equivalent to b, ab, aab, aaab and so on.

Searching a string using Regex

```
1 static void Main(string[] args)

2 {

3 string[] languages = { "C#", "Python", "Java" };

4 foreach(string s in languages)

5 {

6 if(System.Text.RegularExpressions.Regex.IsMatch(s,"Python"))

7 {
```

8 Console.WriteLine("Match found");

9 }

10 }

11 }

The above example searches for "Python" against the set of inputs from the languages array. It uses Regex.IsMatch which returns true in case if the pattern is found in the input. The pattern can be any regular expression representing the input that we want to match.

77. What are the basic String Operations? Explain.

Some of the basic string operations are:

- **Concatenate** –Two strings can be concatenated either by using System.String.Concat or by using + operator.
- **Modify** – Replace(a,b) is used to replace a string with another string. Trim() is used to trim the string at the end or at the beginning.
- **Compare** – System.StringComparison() is used to compare two strings, either case-sensitive comparison or not case sensitive. Mainly takes two parameters, original string, and string to be compared with.
- **Search** – StartWith, EndsWith methods are used to search a particular string.

78. What is Parsing? How to Parse a Date Time String?

Parsing is converting a string into another data type.

For Example:

string text = "500";

int num = int.Parse(text);

500 is an integer. So, Parse method converts the string 500 into its own base type, i.e int.

Follow the same method to convert a DateTime string.

string dateTime = "Jan 1, 2018";

DateTime parsedValue = DateTime.Parse(dateTime);

79. What are Synchronous and Asynchronous operations?

Synchronization is a way to create a thread-safe code where only one thread can access the resource at any given time.

Asynchronous call waits for the method to complete before continuing with the program flow. Synchronous programming badly affects the UI operations, when the user tries to perform time-consuming operations since only one thread will be used.

In Asynchronous operation, the method call will immediately return so that the program can perform other operations while the called method completes its work in certain situations.

80. What is Reflection in C#?

Reflection is the ability of a code to access the metadata of the assembly during runtime. A program reflects upon itself and uses the metadata to inform the user or modify its behavior. Metadata refers to information about objects, methods.

The namespace System.Reflection contains methods and classes that manage the information of all the loaded types and methods. It is mainly used for windows applications, for **Example**, to view the properties of a button in a windows form.

The MemberInfo object of the class reflection is used to discover the attributes associated with a class.

Reflection is implemented in two steps, first, we get the type of the object, and then we use the type to identify members such as methods and properties.

To get type of a class, we can simply use

Type mytype = myClass.GetType();

Once we have a type of class, the other information of the class can be easily accessed.

System.Reflection.MemberInfo Info = mytype.GetMethod*("AddNumbers");*

Above statement tries to find a method with name *AddNumbers* in the class *myClass.*

81. Explain Get and Set Accessor properties?

Get and Set are called Accessors. These are made use by Properties. A property provides a mechanism to read, write the value of a private field. For accessing that private field, these accessors are used.

Get Property is used to return the value of a property
Set Property accessor is used to set the value.

82. What is a Thread? What is Multithreading?

A **Thread** is a set of instructions that can be executed, which will enable our program to perform concurrent processing. Concurrent processing helps us do more than one operation at a time. By default, C# has only one thread. But the other threads can be created to execute the code in parallel with the original thread.

Thread has a life cycle. It starts whenever a thread class is created and is terminated after the execution. *System.Threading* is the namespace which needs to be included to create threads and use its members.

Threads are created by extending the Thread Class. *Start()* method is used to begin thread execution.

//CallThread is the target method//

ThreadStart methodThread = new ThreadStart(CallThread);

Thread childThread = new Thread(methodThread);

childThread.Start();

C# can execute more than one task at a time. This is done by handling different processes by different threads. This is called MultiThreading.

There are several thread methods that are used to handle the multi-threaded operations:

Start, Sleep, Abort, Suspend, Resume and Join.

Most of these methods are self-explanatory.

83. Name some properties of Thread Class.

Few Properties of thread class are:

- **IsAlive** – contains value True when a thread is Active.
- **Name** – Can return the name of the thread. Also, can set a name for the thread.
- **Priority** – returns the prioritized value of the task set by the operating system.
- **IsBackground** – gets or sets a value which indicates whether a thread should be a background process or foreground.
- **ThreadState**– describes the thread state.

84. What are the different states of a Thread?

Different states of a thread are:

- **Unstarted** – Thread is created.
- **Running** – Thread starts execution.
- **WaitSleepJoin** – Thread calls sleep, calls wait on another object and calls join on another thread.
- **Suspended** – Thread has been suspended.
- **Aborted** – Thread is dead but not changed to state stopped.
- **Stopped** – Thread has stopped.

85. What are Async and Await?

Async and Await keywords are used to create asynchronous methods in C.

Asynchronous programming means that the process runs independently of main or other processes.

- Async keyword is used for the method declaration.
- The count is of a task of type int which calls the method CalculateCount().
- Calculatecount() starts execution and calculates something.
- Independent work is done on my thread and then await count statement is reached.
- If the Calculatecount is not finished, myMethod will return to its calling method, thus the main thread doesn't get blocked.
- If the Calculatecount is already finished, then we have the result available when the control reaches await count. So the next step will continue in the same thread. However, it is not the situation in the above case where Delay of 1 second is involved.

86. What is a Deadlock?

A **Deadlock** is a situation where a process is not able to complete its execution because two or more processes are waiting for each other to finish. This usually occurs in multi-threading.

Here a Shared resource is being held by a process and another process is waiting for the first process to release it and the thread holding the locked item is waiting for another process to complete.

87. Explain *Lock, Monitors,* and *Mutex* Object in Threading.

Lock keyword ensures that only one thread can enter a particular section of the code at any given time. In the above **Example**, lock(ObjA) means the lock is placed on ObjA until this process releases it, no other thread can access ObjA.

A **Mutex** is also like a lock but it can work across multiple processes at a time. WaitOne() is used to lock and ReleaseMutex() is used to release the lock. But Mutex is slower than lock as it takes time to acquire and release it.

Monitor.Enter and Monitor.Exit implements lock internally. a lock is a shortcut for **Monitors**. lock(objA) internally calls.

Monitor.Enter(ObjA);

try

{

}

Finally {Monitor.Exit(ObjA));}

88. What is a Race Condition?

A **Race condition** occurs when two threads access the same resource and are trying to change it at the same time. The thread which will be able to access the resource first cannot be predicted.

If we have two threads, T1 and T2, and they are trying to access a shared resource called X. And if both the threads try to write a value to X, the last value written to X will be saved.

89. What is Thread Pooling?

A **Thread pool** is a collection of threads. These threads can be used to perform tasks without disturbing the primary thread. Once the thread completes the task, the thread returns to the pool.

System.Threading.ThreadPool namespace has classes which manage the threads in the pool and its operations.

System.Threading.ThreadPool.QueueUserWorkItem(new System.Threading.WaitCallback(SomeTask));

The above line queues a task. SomeTask methods should have a parameter of type Object.

90. What is Serialization?

When we want to transport an object through a network, then we have to convert the object into a stream of bytes. The process of converting an object into a stream of bytes is called Serialization. For an object to be serializable, it should implement ISerialize Interface. De-serialization is the reverse process of creating an object from a stream of bytes.

Another Explanation for this

Serialization is a process of converting a code to its binary format. Once it is converted to bytes, it can be easily stored and written to a disk or any such storage devices. Serializations are mainly useful when we do not want to lose the original form of the code and it can be retrieved anytime in the future.

Any class which is marked with the attribute [Serializable] will be converted to its binary form.

The reverse process of getting the c# code back from the binary form is called **Deserialization**.

To Serialize an object we need the object to be serialized, a stream which can contain the serialized object and namespace System.Runtime.Serialization can contain classes for serialization.

91. What are the types of Serialization?

The different types of Serialization are: XML serialization, SOAP, and Binary.

- **XML serialization** – It serializes all the public properties to the XML document. Since the data is in XML format, it can be easily read and manipulated in various formats. The classes reside in System.sml.Serialization.
- **SOAP** – Classes reside in System.Runtime.Serialization. Similar to XML but produces a complete SOAP compliant envelope which can be used by any system that understands SOAP.

- **Binary Serialization** – Allows any code to be converted to its binary form. Can serialize and restore public and non-public properties. It is faster and occupies less space.

92. What is an XSD file?

An XSD file stands for XML Schema Definition. It gives a structure for the XML file. It means it decides the elements that the XML should have and in what order and what properties should be present. Without an XSD file associated with XML, the XML can have any tags, any attributes, and any elements.

Xsd.exe tool converts the files to XSD format. During Serialization of C# code, the classes are converted to XSD compliant format by xsd.exe.

C# Professional (Expert)

1.How will you specify what version of the framework your application is targeting?

You can define "targetFramework" in Web.config file to specify the framework version. It is introduced in Asp.net 4.0

1 <?xml version="1.0"?>

2 <configuration>

3 <system.web>

4 <compilation targetFramework="4.0" />

5 </system.web>

6 </configuration>

2. What is the difference between Static class and Singleton instance?

– In c# a static class cannot implement an interface. When a single instance class needs to implement an interface for some business reason or IoC purposes, you can use the Singleton pattern without a static class.
– You can clone the object of Singleton but, you can not clone the static class object
– Singleton object stores in Heap but, static object stores in stack
– A singleton can be initialized lazily or asynchronously while a static class is generally initialized when it is first loaded

3.What is the difference between Unicode,UTF, ASCII and ANSI code format of encoding?

Character encoding interprets the zeros and ones into real characters.

Unicode:

Unicode is a standard that can handle characters for almost all modern languages and even some ancient languages at the same time, as long as the client has fonts for the particular language installed in his system

UTF:

Unicode assigns each character a unique number, or code point. It defines two mapping methods, the UTF (Unicode Transformation Format) encodings, and the UCS (Universal Character Set) encodings. Unicode-based encodings implement the Unicode standard and include UTF-8, UTF-16 and UTF-32/UCS-4. They go beyond 8-bits.

ASCII:

ASCII is abbreviated from American Standard Code for Information Interchange, is a character encoding standard .ASCII codes represent text in computers.It is a code for representing characters as numbers, with each letter assigned a number from 0 to 127.In an ASCII file, each alphabetic, numeric, or special character is represented with a 7-bit binary number

ANSI:

ANSI is abbreviated from American National Standards Institute,is a character encoding standard.ANSI includes all the ASCII characters with an additional 128 character codes. ASCII just defines a 7 bit code page with 128 symbols. ANSI extends this to 8 bit and there are several different code pages for the symbols 128 to 255.

4. Can you serialize hashtable and Why?

No, You can't Serialize Hash table.Because, the .NET Framework does not allow serialization of any object that implements the IDictionary interface

5. What is .PDB file?

PDB is an abbreviation for Program Data Base. It is a repository (persistant storage as databases) to maintain information required to run your program in debug mode. It contains many important relevant information required while debugging your code; for e.g. at what points you have inserted break points where you expect the debugger to break in Visual Studio etc..

6. Why singleton pattern is considered an Anti-pattern ?

– Singletons aren't easy to handle with unit tests. You can't control their instantiation and they may retain state across invocations.
– Memory allocated to an Singleton can't be freed.
– In multithreaded environment, access to the singleton object may have to be guarded (e.g. via synchronization).

– Singletons promote tight coupling between classes, so it is hard to test

7. What are extension methods and where can we use them?

Extension methods enables you to add new capabilities to an existing type. You don't need to make any modifications to the existing type, just bring the extension method into scope and you can call it like a regular instance method. Extension methods need to be declared in a nongeneric, non-nested, static class.

> *Notes:*

- o The difference between a regular static method and an extension method is the special this keyword for the first argument.
- o Extension method cannot be declared on a class or struct.
- o It can also be declared on an interface (such as IEnumerable). Normally, an interface wouldn't have any implementation. With extension methods, however, you can add methods that will be available on every concrete implementation of the interface
- o Language Integrated Query (LINQ) is one of the best examples of how you can use this technique to enhance existing code.

You can read the implementation of Extension Methods in C# here.

8. How to update web.config programatically?

This file is an XML file, and reading/writing XML is supported by .NET. You can choose one of the method as per your requirement:

- o Use System.Xml.XmlDocument class. It implements DOM interface; this way is the easiest and good enough if the size of the document is not too big.
- o Use the classes System.Xml.XmlTextWriter and System.Xml.XmlTextReader; this is the fastest way of reading
- o Use the class System.Xml.Linq.XDocument; this is to support LINQ to XML Programming.

9. What is the difference between Stack and Heap memory in C#?

Stack Memory

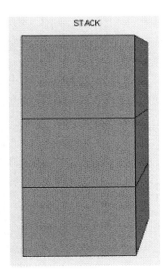

It is an array of memory.

It is a LIFO (Last In First Out) data structure.

In it data can be added to and deleted only from the top of it.

"Things" declared with the following list of type declarations are Value Types

(because they are from System.ValueType):

bool, byte, char, decimal, double, enum, float, int, long, sbyte, short, struct, uint, ulong, ushort

Memory allocation is Static

It is stored Directly

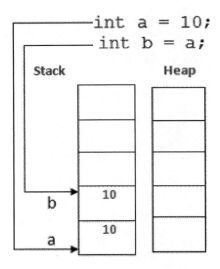

Variables can't be Resized

Its access is fast

Its block allocation is reserved in LIFO.

Most recently reserved block is always the next block to be freed.

It can be visible/accessible only to the Owner Thread

In recursion calls memory filled up quickly

It can be used by one thread of execution

.NET Runtime throws exception "StackOverflowException" when stack space is exhausted

Local variables get wiped off once they lose the scope

It contains values for Integral Types, Primitive Types and References to the Objects.

Heap Memory

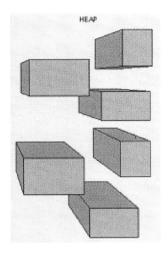

It is an area of memory where chunks are allocated to store certain kinds of data objects.

In it data can be stored and removed in any order.

"Things" declared with following list of type declarations are Reference Types

(and inherit from System.Object... except, of course, for object which is the System.Object object):

class, interface, delegate, object, string

Memory allocation is Dynamic

It is stored indirectly

```
string s = "Hello";
string ss = s;
```

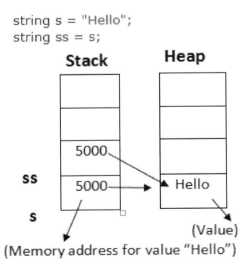

Variables can be Resized

Its access is Slow

Its block allocation is free and done at any time

It can be visible/accessible to all the threads

In recursion calls memory filled up slowly

It can be used by all the parts of the application

It is a special thread created by .NET runtime to monitor allocations of heap space.

It only collects heap memory since objects are only created in heap

10. What is the difference between covariance and contravariance?

If you have an interface IFoo<T> it can be covariant in T (i.e. declare it as IFoo<out T> if T is only used in an output position (e.g. a return type) within the interface. It can be contravariant in T (i.e. IFoo<in T>) if T is only used in an input position (e.g. a parameter type).

Covariance

Canonical examples: IEnumerable<out T>, Func<out T>

You can convert from IEnumerable<string> to IEnumerable<object>, or Func<string> to Func<object>. Values only come *out from* these objects.

It works because if you're only taking values out of the API, and it's going to return something specific (like string), you can treat that returned value as a more general type (like object).

Contravariance

Canonical examples: IComparer<in T>, Action<in T>

You can convert from IComparer<object> to IComparer<string>,
or Action<object> to Action<string>; values only go *into* these objects.

This time it works because if the API is expecting something general
(like object) you can give it something more specific (like string).

11. What are indexers in C# .NET? What is the difference between property & indexers?

An indexer is a pair of get and set accessors, similar to those of properties.

- Like a property, an indexer does not allocate memory for storage.
- Both indexers and properties are used primarily for giving access to other data members with which they are associated and for which they provide get and set access.
  – A property usually represents a single data member.
  – An indexer usually represents multiple data members.
- Like a property, an indexer can have either one or both of the accessors.
- Indexers are always instance members; hence, an indexer cannot be declared static.
- Like properties, the code implementing the get and set accessors does not have to be associated with any fields or properties. The code can do anything, or nothing, as long as the get accessor returns some value of the specified type.

12. What's difference between delegate and events?

An event is just a wrapper for a multicast delegate.
Adding a public event to a class is almost the same as adding a public multicast delegate field.
In both cases, subscriber objects can register for notifications, and in both cases the publisher object can send notifications to the subscribers. However, a public multicast delegate has the undesirable property that external objects can invoke the delegate, something we'd normally want to restrict to the publisher. Hence events – an event adds public methods to the containing class to add and

remove receivers, but does not make the invocation mechanism public.

13. Can we Overload main() method in C#?

Yes, We can overload main() method. A C# class can have any number of main() methods.
But to run the C# class, class should have main() method with signature as "public static void main(String⬚ args)". If you do any modification to this signature, compilation will be successful. But, You will get run time error as main method not found.

14. How to design a class (or data type) which sorts its data either ascending or descending by default

You can do this by using Array.BinarySearch. Below is the implementation in C#.

```
1  class Program

2     {

3         static void Main(string⬚ args)

4         {

5             MySortedList list = new MySortedList();

6         list.Add(13);

7         list.Add(81);

8         list.Add(25);

9         list.Add(9);

10        list.Add(33);
```

```
11        list.Add(46);

12        list.Add(1);

13        foreach (int v in list.Items)

14          {

15            Console.WriteLine(v);

16          }

17        Console.ReadLine();

18      }

19    }

20

21    class MySortedList

22    {

23      int[] items = new int[0];

24      public int[] Items

25      {

26        get { return items; }

27        set { items = value; }

28      }

29

30      public void Add(int value)
```

```
31      {
32          int index = Array.BinarySearch(items, value);
33          if (index < 0)
34              index = ~index;
35
36          //Increase Items Array Size by 1
37          int lastIndex = items.Length;
38          int capacity = items.Length + 1;
39          int[] dupArray = new int[capacity];
40          Array.Copy(items, dupArray, items.Length);
41          items = dupArray;
42
43          //Adjusting elements to insert element in its right index
44          if (index < lastIndex)
45          {
46              Array.Copy(items, index, items, index + 1, lastIndex - index);
47          }
48          items[index] = value;
49      }
50  }
```

15.You have a component with 5 parameters and deployed to client side now you changed your method which takes 6 parameters. How can you deploy this without affecting the client's code?

Instead of adding 6th parameter to the existing method, write new overloaded method with 6 parameters.

So when old application calls this method, method with 5 parameter will execute.
And method with 6 parameter will be used by new application. That way we can provide backward compatibility to old application.

16. What is Satellite Assembly?

A satellite assembly is a compiled library (DLL) that contains "localizable" resources specific to a given culture such as strings, bitmaps, etc. You are likely to use satellite assemblies when creating a multilingual UI application.

As per MSDN definition, A .NET Framework assembly containing resources specific to a given language. Using satellite assemblies, you can place the resources for different languages in different assemblies, and the correct assembly is loaded into memory only if the user elects to view the application in that language.

17.Explain the difference between Error and Exception in C#?

Exception handling is a mechanism to detect and handle error at run time where as Errors are occured at development/compile time.
You can read more on exception handling in C# here.

18. What is the difference between == and .Equals method in c#?

int x = 20;

int y = 20;

Console.WriteLine(x == y);

Console.WriteLine(x.Equals(y));

Output:

True

True

For Reference Type:

== performs an identity comparison, i.e. it will only return true if both references point to the same object. While **Equals**() method is expected to perform a value comparison, i.e. it will return true if the references point to objects that are equivalent.

For Example:
StringBuilder s1 = new StringBuilder("Yes");

StringBuilder s2 = new StringBuilder("Yes");

Console.WriteLine(s1 == s2);

Console.WriteLine(s1.Equals(s2));

Output:

False

True

In above example, s1 and s2 are different objects hence "==" returns false, but they are equivalent hence "Equals()" method returns true. Remember there is an exception of this rule, i.e. when you use "==" operator with string class it compares value rather than identity.

When to use "==" operator and when to use ".Equals()" method?

For value comparison, with Value Type use "==" operator and use "Equals()" method while performing value comparison with Reference Type.

5. What is Partial class and What all are the What is Partial class and What all are the advantages of Partial class

19.What is Partial class and What all are the advantages of Partial class?

The class declaration can be partitioned into several partial class declarations.

o   Each of the partial class declarations contains the declarations of some of the class members.
o   The partial class declarations of a class can be in the same file or in different files.
o   Each partial declaration must be labeled as partial class,in contrast to the single keyword class.

Advantages of Partial Class:

By Using Partial Classes, multiple developer can work on the same class easily. Partial classes are mainly used by code generator to keep different concerns separate
you can also define Partial methods as well where a developer can simply define the method and the other developer can implement that.

20. What all are the Advantages and Disadvantages of Generics in C#?

Advantages of Generics:

o   Generics provide type safety without the overhead of multiple implementations.
o   Generics eliminates boxing and unboxing.

o There is no need to write code to test for the correct data type because it is enforced at compile time. The need for type casting and the possibility of run-time errors are reduced.

o By providing strong typing, a class built from a generic lets visual studio provide IntelliSense.

o Generic collection types generally perform better for storing and manipulating value types because there is no need to box the value types

o Generic delegates enable type-safe callbacks without the need to create multiple delegate classes.

Disdvantages of Generics:

☐ Generic types can be derived from most base classes, such as MarshalByRefObject (and constraints can be used to require that generic type parameters derive from base classes like MarshalByRefObject). However, the .NET Framework does not support context-bound generic types. A generic type can be derived from ContextBoundObject, but trying to create an instance of that type causes a TypeLoadException.

☐ Enumerations cannot have generic type parameters.

☐ Lightweight dynamic methods cannot be generic.

☐ In C#, a nested type that is enclosed in a generic type cannot be instantiated unless types have been assigned to the type parameters of all enclosing types

21. Why C# main method is static?

The C# main method is static because object is not required to call static method if it were non-static method, compiler creates object first then call main() method that will lead the problem of extra memory allocation.

22. What is Implementation Inheritance and Interface Inheritance?

Implementation inheritance:

– It is achieved when a class is derived from another class in such a way that it inherits all its members.
– It is called as Class Inheritance.

– In this, it uses 'extends' keyword in Java.
– The subclass is tightly coupled with superclass.
– If there is any changes to superclass will break the whole relationship.

Interface inheritance:

– It is achieved when a class inherits only the signatures of the functions from another class.
– It is called as Type inheritance and also called as subtyping.
– In this, it uses 'implements' keyword in Java.
– It is used for code reuse and polymorphism.
– It reduces coupling and implementation dependencies.

23. What is Assembly Manifest?

Within every Assembly there is an Assembly Manifest. It contains:
-The assembly's identity (its name and version).
-A file table describing all the other files that make up the assembly, for example, any other assemblies you created that your .exe or .dll file relies on, or even bitmap or Readme files.
-An assembly reference list, which is a list of all external dependencies—.dlls or other files your application needs that may have been created by someone else. Assembly references contain references to both global and private objects. Global objects reside in the global assembly cache.

24. What is Reflection and what all are the common use of Reflection?

Reflection is a process by which a program can examine and manipulate program objects at run time.
Common use of Reflection:

– Load assemblies at runtime
– it allows you to learn what assembly defines a particular item such as a class or enumeration
– List a class's field,properties, constructors, event and methods
– Get information about a property such as type and if it is read only
– Get and Set property's value
– Get information about item's attribute etc..

25. What is Encapsulation and Data hiding in C#?

– Encapsulation is a process of hiding the members from outside of class and implemented using access specifiers
– Encapsulation is also called as information hiding.
– Encapsulation provides a way to preserve the integrity of state data. Rather than defining public fields, private data fields should be defined.
– Well-encapsulated class should hide its data and the details of how it operates on data from the outside world. This is termed black box programming.
– Using this,implementation of the method can be changed by the class author without breaking any existing code making use of it.

26. What does the tilde (~) mean in C#?

The ~ operator performs a bitwise complement operation on its operand, which has the effect of reversing each bit. Bitwise complement operators are predefined for int, uint, long, and ulong. Also the ~ symbol is used to declare destructors.

You can read more on tilde(~) here.

27. Can you use tilde(~) with Enum in C# ?

Yes, You can use tilde(~) with Enum to flips the bits of its operand.

```
1  //using tilde(~)

2  [Flags]

3  public enum PurchaseMethod

4  {

5      All = ~0,

6      None =  0,
```

```
7      Cash =  1,

8      Check =  2,

9      CreditCard =  4

10 }

11 //Alternative:

12 [Flags]

13 public enum PurchaseMethod

14 {

15     None = 0,

16     Cash = 1,

17     Check = 2,

18     CreditCard = 4,

19     All = Cash | Check | CreditCard

20 }
```

– Source: Stack Overflow

28. What does placing a @ in front of a C# variable name do?

It's a way to allow declaring reserved keywords as vars.
Example

```
1 void test(int @string)
```

29.How do you give a C# Auto-Property a default value?

In C#5 and earlier, you can do it using constructor.

```
1 class Employee
2 {
3    public Employee()
4    {
5       Name = "Default Name";
6    }
7    public string Name { get; set; }
8 }
```

In C#6.0, You can do:

public string Name { get; set; } = "Default Name"

30. What is the use of Yield keyword in C#?

Yield keyword helps us to do custom stateful iteration over .NET collections. There are two scenarios where "yield" keyword is useful:-
− It helps to provide custom iteration without creating temp collections.
− It helps to do state-full iteration

31. What is AsyncCallback in C#?

When the async method finishes the processing, AsyncCallback method is automatically called, where post processing stmts can be executed. With this technique there is no need to poll or wait for the async thread to complete.

32. What is Nested types in C# and how to use it?

Types are usually declared directly inside a namespace. You can, however, also declare types inside a class or struct declaration.
– Types declared inside another type declaration are called nested types. Like all type declarations, nested types are templates for an instance of the type.
– A nested type is declared like a member of the enclosing type.
– A nested type can be any type.
– An enclosing type can be either a class or a struct.

For example, the following code shows class MyClass, with a nested class called MyCounter.

```
1 class MyClass // Enclosing class

2  {

3    class MyCounter // Nested class

4    {

5      ...

6    }

7    ...

8  }
```

It is good to use Nested types if it is only meant to be used as a helper for the enclosing type.

attributes.

33. What is Null Coalescing Operator in C#?

C# Supports a special operator called the null coalescing operator, which returns a non-null value to an expression, in case a nullable type variable is null. The null coalescing operator consists of two contiguous question marks and has two operands.
– The first operand is a variable of a nullable type.
– The second is a non-nullable value of the underlying type.
– If, at run time, the first operand (the nullable operand) evaluates to null, the nonnullable operand is returned as the result of the expression.
Example:

```
1   int? myI4 = null;

2   Console.WriteLine("myI4: {0}", myI4 ?? -1);

3   myI4 = 10;

4   Console.WriteLine("myI4: {0}", myI4 ?? -1);
```

This code produces the following output:

1 myI4: –1

2 myI4: 10

34. What are weakreferences in C#?How is it different than StrongReferences

The garbage collector cannot collect an object in use by an application while the application's code can reach that object. The application is said to have a strong reference to the object.
A weak reference permits the garbage collector to collect the object while still allowing the application to access the object. A weak reference is valid only during the indeterminate amount of time until the object is collected when no strong references exist. When you use a weak reference, the application can still obtain a strong reference to the object, which prevents it from being collected. However, there is always the risk that the garbage collector will get to the object first before a strong reference is re-established.

Weak references are useful for objects that use a lot of memory, but can be recreated easily if they are reclaimed by garbage collection

35. What are XML namespaces for?

XML namespaces are like packages in C#.They are for allowing multiple markup languages to be combined, without having to worry about conflicts of element and attribute names.
– You can reuse a set of tags/attributes you define across different types of xml documents.
– If you need to add some "aspect" to your XML; adding a namespace to your xml document is simpler than changing your whole xml schema definition.
– Avoid poluting the "main" namespace: You don't force your parser to work with a huge schema definition, just use the namespace you need to.

36. What is the difference between string and String in C# ?

String stands for System.String and it is a .NET Framework type. string is an alias in the C# language for System.String. Both of them are compiled to System.String in IL (Intermediate Language), so there is no difference.

37. What's the difference between the 'ref' and 'out' keywords in C#?

The ref modifier means that:
– The value is already set and
– The method can read and modify it.
The out modifier means that:
– The Value isn't set and can't be read by the method until it is set.
– The method must set it before returning.

semantically, ref provides both "in" and "out" functionality, whereas out only provides "out" functionality.

38. What is the difference between myEmployee.GetType() and typeof(Employee) in C#?

The result of both would be exactly the same. It will be your Employee type that derives from System.Type. The only real difference here is that when you want to obtain the type from an instance of your class, you use GetType. If you don't have an instance, but you know the type name, you would use typeof.
GetType gets resolved at runtime, while typeof is resolved at compile time.

39. What is the difference between an EXE and a DLL?

EXE:
– Executable file, can run independently
– It runs in a separate process
– It can't be reused in application
– it has a main function
DLL:
– Dynamic link library is used as part of EXE or other DLL's
– It runs in application process memory,
– It can be reused in application
– It does not have a main function

40. What are the advantages and disadvantages of using the GAC?

– GAC is a central repository in a system in which assemblies are registered to shared between application.
– GACUtil.exe is used to view and change the content of GAC in system
– GAC can contain multiple versions on .net assemblies
– Thegautil.exe/I is used to install assembly in GAC

Advantages & Disadvantages:
– Loading assemblies from GAC mean less overhead and security that your application will always load correct version of .NET library
– You shouldn't ngen assemblies that are outside of GAC, because there will be almost no performance gain, in many cases even loss in performance.
– You're already using GAC, because all standard .NET assemblies are actually in GAC and ngened (during installation).
– Using GAC for your own libraries adds complexity into deployment, I would try to avoid it at all costs.
– Your users need to be logged as administrators during installation if you want to put something into GAC, quite a problem for many types of applications.

41. What is the difference between a process and a thread?

Process:
— An executing instance of a program is called a process.
— Some operating systems use the term 'task' to refer to a program that is being executed.
— A process is always stored in the main memory also termed as the primary memory or random access memory.
— Therefore, a process is termed as an active entity. It disappears if the machine is rebooted.
— Several process may be associated with a same program.
— On a multiprocessor system, multiple processes can be executed in parallel.
— On a uni-processor system, though true parallelism is not achieved, a process scheduling algorithm is applied and the processor is scheduled to execute each process one at a time yielding an illusion of concurrency.

Thread:
— A thread is a subset of the process.
— It is termed as a 'lightweight process', since it is similar to a real process but executes within the context of a process and shares the same resources allotted to the process by the kernel.
— Usually, a process has only one thread of control — one set of machine instructions executing at a time.
— A process may also be made up of multiple threads of execution that execute instructions concurrently.
— Multiple threads of control can exploit the true parallelism possible on multiprocessor systems.
— On a uni-processor system, a thread scheduling algorithm is applied and the processor is scheduled to run each thread one at a time.
— All the threads running within a process share the same address space, file descriptors, stack and other process related attributes.
— Since the threads of a process share the same memory, synchronizing the access to the shared data withing the process gains unprecedented importance.

— Source: Knowledge Quest

42. If asynchronous execution takes less total time to finish than synchronous execution, why would anybody choose synchronous execution?

In Synchronus mode, every task executes in sequence, so it's easier to program. That's the way we've been doing it for years.

With asynchronous execution, you have few challenges:
– You must synchronize tasks. for e.g. you run a task that must be executed after the other three have finished. You will have to create a mechanism to wait for all tasks to finish before launching the new task.
– You must address concurrency issues. If you have a shared resource, like a list that is written in one task and read in another, make sure that it's kept in a known state.
– There is no logical sequence anymore. The tasks can end at any time, and you don't have control of which one finishes first.

But in synchronous programming we have below disadvantages:
– It takes longer to finish.
– It may stop the user interface (UI) thread. Typically, these programs have only one UI thread, and when you use it as a blocking operation, you get the spinning wheel (and "not responding" in the caption title) in your program— not the best experience for your users.
It doesn't use the multicore architecture of the new processors. Regardless of whether your program is running on a 1-core or a 64-core processor, – it will run as quickly (or slowly) on both.
Asynchronous programming eliminates these disadvantages: it won't hang the UI thread (because it can run as a background task), and it can use all the cores in your machine and make better use of machine resources. So, do you choose easier programming or better use of resources? Fortunately, you don't have to make this decision. Microsoft has created several ways to minimize the difficulties of programming for asynchronous execution.

43. Why do we need C# delegates?

you can call methods directly on the object but in below scenarios you may consider using Delegates:
– You want to call series of method by using single delegate without writing lot

of method calls.
– You want to implement event based system elegantly.
– You want to call two methods same in signature but reside in different classes.
– You want to pass method as a parameter.
– You don't want to write lot of polymorphic code like in LINQ , you can provide lot of implementation to the Select method.

44. why do we use the Dictionary class instead of the Hashtable class?

Dictionary is a generic type, Hashtable is not. That means you get type safety with Dictionary, because you can't insert any random object into it, and you don't have to cast the values you take out.

Hashtable supports multiple reader threads with a single writer thread, while Dictionary offers no thread safety. If you need thread safety with a generic dictionary, you must implement your own synchronization.

45. Are nullable types reference types in C# ?

Nullable types are instances of the System.Nullable struct.Nullable types represent value-type variables that can be assigned the value of null. You cannot create a nullable type based on a reference type. So nullable types are not reference types.

46. What is the difference between System exceptions and Application exceptions?

System exceptions are derived directly from a base class System.SystemException. A System level Exception is normally thrown when a nonrecoverable error has occurred.
Application exceptions can be user defined exceptions thrown by the applications. If you are designing an application that needs to create its own exceptions class, you are advised to derive custom exceptions from the System.ApplicationException class. It is typically thrown when a recoverable error has occurred.

47. What is the difference between Var and Dynamics in C#?

Dynamic

Introduced in C# 4.0

Dynamically typed – This means the type of variable declared is decided by the compiler at run time.

No need to initialize at the time of declaration.

e.g., dynamic str;

Looking at the value assigned to the variable str, the compiler will treat the variable str as string.   str="I am a string"; //Works fine and compiles

Errors are caught at runtime

Since the compiler comes to about the type and the methods and properties of the type at the run time.

Intellisense help is not available for dynamic type of variables since their type is unknown until run time. So intellisense help is not available. Even if you are informed by the compiler as "This operation will be resolved at run-time".

Will compile

var

Introduced in C# 3.0

Statically typed – This means the type of variable declared is decided by the compiler at compile time.

var type of variables are required to be initialized at the time of declaration or else they encounter the compile time error: Implicitly-typed local variables must be initialized.

e.g., var str="I am a string";

Errors are caught at compile time.

Since the compiler knows about the type and the methods and properties of the type at the compile time itself

Intellisense help is available for the var type of variables. This is because, its type is inferred by the compiler from the type of value it is assigned and as a result, the compiler has all the information related to the type

will throw a compile error since the variable is not initialized. The compiler needs that this variable should be initialized so that it can infer a type from the value.

48. When to use Tuples in C#?

Tuples are commonly used in four ways:

– To represent a single set of data. For example, a tuple can represent a database record, and its components can represent individual fields of the record.
– To provide easy access to, and manipulation of, a data set.
– To return multiple values from a method without using out parameters
– To pass multiple values to a method through a single parameter. For example, the Thread.Start(Object) method has a single parameter that lets you supply one value to the method that the thread executes at startup time. If you supply a Tuple object as the method argument, you can supply the thread's startup routine with three items of data.

49. How can you create responsive UI without impacting users?

You can create a responsive UI using multithreading. You can split the work into small pieces and run it in background without impacting user.

50. How to Force Garbage Collection?

You can force this by adding a call to GC.Collect.
Example:

1 StreamWriter stream = File.CreateText("temp.dat");

2 stream.Write("some test data");

3 GC.Collect();

4 GC.WaitForPendingFinalizers();

5 File.Delete("temp.dat");

51. What is the difference between Lock and Monitor in C#?

Monitor and lock is the way to provide thread safety in a multithreaded application in C#.Lock is the keyword in C# that will ensure one thread is executing a piece of code at one time. The lock keyword ensures that one thread does not enter a critical section of code while another thread is in that critical section.

52. Why do we need Reflection in C#?

We use Reflection in C#:
– Load assemblies at runtime
– it allows you to learn what assembly defines a particular item such as a class or enumeration
– List a class's field,properties, constructors, event and methods
– Get information about a property such as type and if it is read only
– Get and Set property's value
– Get information about item's attribute etc..

53.How do you mark a method as Obsolete/Deprecated?

You can use Obsolete attribute to mark a method as Obsolete or Deprecated

54.Can you use ref and out parameters in Lambda expression, if declared outside?

If you will use ref or out parameter outside of Lamda Expression then you will get compile time error.

```
1    static void DoWork(int valIn, out int valOut)

2        {

3          int local;

4

5          Action doCalc = () =>

6            {

7              local = valIn * 2;   // this will work fine

8              //valOut = valIn * i;  // this will be a compile time error

9            };

10

11         // you can use the out parameter to assign result of lambda

12         Func<int> doCalc2 = () => valIn * 2;

13         valOut = doCalc2();   // Allowed

14       }
```

55. How to return multiple values from a function in C#?

In C#, There are several ways to return multiple values from a C# function.

– Using KeyValue pair
– Using ref/out parameters
– Using Struct or Class
– Using Tuple

of arrays.

56. How can you cancel an Async operation in C#?

You can cancel your own async operation. There are two classes in the System.Threading.Tasks namespace that are designed for this purpose: CancellationToken and CancellationTokenSource.

A CancellationToken object contains the information about whether a task should be cancelled or not.
A task that has a CancellationToken object needs to periodically inspect it to see what the token's state is. If the CancellationToken object's IsCancellationRequested property is set to true, the task should halt its operations and return.
A CancellationToken is nonreversible and can only be used once. That is, once it's IsCancellationRequested property is set to true, it can't be changed.
A CancellationTokenSource object creates a CancellationToken object, which can then be given to various tasks. Any objects holding a cancellationTokenSource can call its Cancel method, which sets the CancellationToken's IsCancellationRequested property to true.

57. Can abstract class be Sealed in C#?

An abstract class cannot be a sealed class because the sealed modifier prevents a class from being inherited and the abstract modifier requires a class to be inherited.

58. What is the main use of a finally block in exception handling?

The finally block is linked with a try block and contains a block of statements that are executed irrespective of whether an exception occurs
or not within the try block. Finally defines the code that is executed always.
In the normal execution it is executed after the try block When an exception occurs, it is executed after the handler if any or before propagation as the case may be.

59. How to avoid Singleton instance creation by cloning ?

We can create a copy of an object using clone() method.

To avoid creating a clone of our singleton class, we can do the following :
− Implement MethodwiseClone()
− Override the clone() method and throw CloneNotSupportedException from it.

```
1  protected object MemberwiseClone()

2  {

3      throw new Exception("Cloning a singleton object is not allowed");

4  }
```

60. What are generations in GC?

After the garbage collector is initialized by the CLR, it allocates a segment of memory to store and manage objects.

This memory is called the managed heap, as opposed to a native heap in the operating system.

There is a managed heap for each managed process. All threads in the process allocate memory for objects on the same heap.

The heap is organized into generations so it can handle long-lived and short-lived objects. Garbage collection primarily occurs with the reclamation of short-lived objects that typically occupy only a small part of the heap. There are three generations of objects on the heap:

Generation 0. This is the youngest generation and contains short-lived objects. An example of a short-lived object is a temporary variable. Garbage collection occurs most frequently in this generation.

Newly allocated objects form a new generation of objects and are implicitly generation 0 collections, unless they are large objects, in which case they go on the large object heap in a generation 2 collection.

Most objects are reclaimed for garbage collection in generation 0 and do not survive to the next generation.
Generation 1. This generation contains short-lived objects and serves as a buffer between short-lived objects and long-lived objects.
Generation 2. This generation contains long-lived objects. An example of a long-lived object is an object in a server application that contains static data that is live for the duration of the process.

Garbage collections occur on specific generations as conditions warrant. Collecting a generation means collecting objects in that generation and all its younger generations. A generation 2 garbage collection is also known as a full garbage collection, because it reclaims all objects in all generations (that is, all objects in the managed heap).

Generation 0 – Short-lived Objects
Generation 1- As a buffer between short lived and long lived objects
Generation 2 – Long lived objects

61. How to catch multiple exceptions at once in C#?

You can catch multiple exceptions using condition statements in C#.
Example

```
1  catch (Exception ex)

2  {

3     if (ex is FormatException || ex is OverflowException)

4     {

5        testid = "";

6        return;
```

```
7    }

8

9    throw;

10 }

1    catch (Exception ex) when (ex is FormatException || ex is
     OverflowException)

2    {

3      testid = "";

4      return;

5    }
```

62. Write a Regular expression to validate email address?

$\wedge[a\text{-}zA-Z0-9\,.\_\%+\text{-}]+@[a\text{-}zA-Z0\text{-}9\,.\_\%+\text{-}]+\backslash.[a\text{-}zA\text{-}Z]\{2,4\}\$$

In the above example:
– the sequence $\wedge[a\text{-}zA-Z0-9\,.\_\%+\text{-}]$ matches letters,digits,underscores,%,+ and -.
– The + (plus) sign after the 1st sequence means the string must include one or more of those characters
– Next the pattern matches @
– Then the pattern matches another letter one or more times followed by a . and then between two to four letters

63. Can you loop through all Enum values in C#?

Yes, you can loop through all Enum values using GetValues or the typed version.

```
1 public enum Color {
```

2   Red,

3   Blue,

4   Black,

5   White

6 }

7 var values = Enum.GetValues(typeof(Colors));

8 //Or the typed version

9 var values = Enum.GetValues(typeof(Colors)).Cast<Colors>();

64. Should 'using' statements be inside or outside the namespace in C#?

Let's look at below example to understand the difference of 'using' statements inside or outside the namespace.
suppose there are 2 files.

```
1  // File1.cs

2  using System;

3  namespace Outer.Inner

4  {

5      class Foo

6      {

7          static void Bar()

8          {
```

```
9         double d = Math.PI;

10      }

11    }

12 }

13

14 // File2.cs

15 namespace Outer

16 {

17    class Math

18    {

19    }

20 }
```

The compiler searches Outer before looking at those using statements outside the namespace, so it finds Outer.Math instead of System.Math. Outer.Math has no PI member, so File1 is now broken.

This changes if you put the "using" inside your namespace declaration, as follows:

```
1  // File1b.cs

2  namespace Outer.Inner

3  {
```

```
4    using System;

5    class Foo

6    {

7       static void Bar()

8       {

9          double d = Math.PI;

10      }

11   }

12 }
```

Now the compiler searches 'System' before searching 'Outer', finds 'System.Math'. So this will work fine.

So we can say it depends on the type of system we are creating.

65. Should a return statement be inside or outside a lock statement?

Whether you put the return statement inside or outside a lock statement, It doesn't make any difference; they're both translated to the same thing by the compiler.

It is recommended to put the return inside the lock. Otherwise you risk another thread entering the lock and modifying your variable before the return statement, therefore making the original caller receive a different value than expected.

66. How to iterate over a Dictionary in C#?

You can use keyValue pair to iterate over a dictionary in C#.

```
foreach(KeyValuePair<string, string> entry in myDic)

{

    // do something with entry.Value or entry.Key

}
```

If you are trying to use a generic Dictionary in C# like you would use an associative array in another language:

```
foreach(var item in myDictionary)

{

  foo(item.Key);

  bar(item.Value);

}
```

Or, if you only need to iterate over the collection of keys, use

```
foreach(var item in myDictionary.Keys)

{

  foo(item);

}
```

And lastly, if you're only interested in the values:

```
foreach(var item in myDictionary.Values)

{
```

NET Interview Questions for Freshers and Experienced

```
foo(item);

}
```

67. What is the use of the IDisposable interface in C#

The primary use of the IDisposable interface is to clean up unmanaged resources."unmanaged" means things like database connections, sockets, window handles, etc.The garbage collector doesn't know how to call DeleteHandle() on a variable of type IntPtr, it doesn't know whether or not it needs to call DeleteHandle().

So Microsoft has faciliated the Idisposable Interface and Dispose method to clean up unmanaged resources.

Implement IDisposable and Dispose method:

```
1  using System;

2  using System.IO;

3  class UnmangedWrapper : IDisposable

4  {

5  public FileStream Stream { get; private set; }

6     public UnmangedWrapper()

7      {

8        this.Stream = File.Open("temp.dat", FileMode.Create);

9      }

10    ~UnmangedWrapper()
```

```
11      {

12          Dispose(false);

13      }

14 public void Close()

15  {

16      Dispose();

17  }

18 public void Dispose()

19  {

20      Dispose(true);

21      System.GC.SuppressFinalize(this);

22  }

23 public void Dispose(bool disposing)

24  {

25      if (disposing)

26      {

27          if (Stream != null)

28          {

29              Stream.Close();

30          }
```

31   }

32   }

33 }

68. What all are the difference between Dictionary class and Hashtable class?

Hashtable

A Hashtable is a non-generic collection.

Hashtable is defined under System.Collections namespace.

In Hashtable, you can store key/value pairs of the same type or of the different type.

In Hashtable, there is no need to specify the type of the key and value.

The data retrieval is slower than Dictionary due to boxing/ unboxing.

In Hashtable, if you try to access a key that doesn't present in the given Hashtable, then it will give null values.

It is thread safe.

It doesn't maintain the order of stored values.

Dictionary

A Dictionary is a generic collection.

Dictionary is defined under System.Collections.Generic namespace.

In Dictionary, you can store key/value pairs of same type.

In Dictionary, you must specify the type of key and value.

The data retrieval is faster than Hashtable due to no boxing/ unboxing.

In Dictionary, if you try to access a key that doesn't present in the given Dictionary, then it will give error.

It is also thread safe but only for public static members.

It always maintain the order of stored values.

69. When to use struct instead of class in C#?

Consider defining a structure instead of a class if instances of the type are small and commonly short-lived or are commonly embedded in other objects.
Do not define a structure unless the type has all of the following characteristics:
– It logically represents a single value, similar to primitive types (integer, double, and so on).
– It has an instance size smaller than 16 bytes.
– It is immutable.
– It will not have to be boxed frequently.

70.How do you generate a random number in C#?

The Random class is used to create random numbers in C#.

```
1 //Example:

2 Random r = new Random();

3 int n = r.Next();
```

71. How to split string using Regex in C#?

The Regular Expressions Split() methods are similar to the String.Split() method, except that Regex.Split() method splits the string at a delimiter determined by a Regular Expression instead of a set of characters.

When using Regular Expressions you should use the following namespace:

```
1 using System.Text.RegularExpressions;

2 string str = "test1\n  \ntest2\n  \ntest3\n  \n  \ntest4";
```

```
3  string[] result = Regex.Split(str, "\n\\s*");

4  for (int i = 0; i < result.Length; i++)

5     MessageBox.Show(result[i]);

6

7  //Output:

8  test1

9  test2

10 test3

11 test4
```

72. How can you get the assembly version in C#?

You can get the assembly version in C#:

```
1 Version version = Assembly.GetEntryAssembly().GetName().Version;
```

73.How would you Read settings from app.config or web.config in C#?

```
ConfigurationManager.AppSettings["MySetting"]
```

You will need to add a reference to System.Configuration in your project's references folder.

74. When you create and compile an application in C#, what all are the files get generated in Debug folder?

When you will create and compile a program in C#, you will see below files in Debug folder.
– exe – the 'normal' executable
– vshost.exe – a special version of the executable to aid debuging; see MSDN for details
– pdb – the Program Data Base with debug symbols
– vshost.exe.manifest – a kind of configuration file containing mostly dependencies on libraries

75.Can you add extension methods to an existing static class?

No. Extension methods require an instance of an object. However, you can do something like this:

```
1   public static class Extensions
2   {
3       public static T Create<T>(this T @this)
4           where T : class, new()
5       {
6           return Utility<T>.Create();
7       }
8   }
9
10  public static class Utility<T>
```

```
   where T : class, new()
   {
       static Utility()
       {
           Create =
Expression.Lambda<Func<T>>(Expression.New(typeof(T).GetConstructor(
Type.EmptyTypes))).Compile();
       }
   public static Func<T> Create { get; private set; }
}
```

76. What is the difference between Object pooling and Connection pooling in C#?

The object pool implementation will increase the size of the pool up to the specified maximum. When the maximum is reached,instead of throwing an exception, it makes the client wait until an object is returned to the pool, and then gives the newly returned object to the waiting client.

The connection pool implementation does not have a maximum size parameter – it will keep creating new connections to meet demand (eventually it will hit some system limit and the request will fail in some way that isn't specified.

77. What is the use of volatile keyword?

The volatile keyword indicates that a field might be modified by multiple threads that are executing at the same time. Fields that are declared volatile are not subject to compiler optimizations that assume access by a single thread. This ensures that the most up-to-date value is present in the field at all times. The volatile modifier is usually used for a field that is accessed by multiple threads without using the lock statement to serialize access.
The volatile keyword can be applied to fields of these types:
– Reference types.
– Pointer types (in an unsafe context). Note that although the pointer itself can be volatile, the object that it points to cannot. In other words, you cannot declare a "pointer to volatile."
– Integral types such as sbyte, byte, short, ushort, int, uint, char, float, and bool.
– An enum type with an integral base type.
– Generic type parameters known to be reference types.
– IntPtr and UIntPtr.

78. What is the use of Partial class in C#?

– By Using Partial Classes, multiple developer can work on the same class easily.
– Partial classes are mainly used by code generator to keep different concerns separate
– you can also define Partial methods as well where a developer can simply define the method and the other developer can implement that.

Explain Constructor Overloading, **Constructor Chaining, copy constructor**

It is quite similar to the Method overloading. It is the ability to redefine a Constructor in more than one form. A user can implement constructor overloading by defining two or more constructors in a class sharing the same name. C# can distinguish the constructors with different signatures. i.e. the constructor must have the same name but with different parameters list.

We can overload constructors in different ways as follows:

- By using different **type of arguments**
- By using different **number of arguments**
- By using different **order of arguments**

By changing the Data types of the parameters

Example:

```
public ADD (int a, float b);

public ADD (string a, int b);
```

Here the name of the class is **ADD**. In first constructor there are two parameters, first one is **int** and another one is **float** and in second constructor, also there is two parameters, first one is **string** type and another one is **int** type. Here the constructors have the same name but the types of the parameters are different, similar to the concept of method overloading.

```
// C# program to Demonstrate the overloading of
// constructor when the types of arguments
// are different
usingSystem;

classADD {

    intx, y;
    doublef;
    strings;

    // 1st constructor
    publicADD(inta, doubleb)
    {
        x = a;
        f = b;
    }

    // 2nd constructor
    publicADD(inta, stringb)
    {
        y = a;
        s = b;
```

```
}

// showing 1st constructor's result
publicvoidshow()
{
    Console.WriteLine("1st constructor (int + float): {0} ",
                        (x + f));
}

// shows 2nd constructor's result
publicvoidshow1()
{
    Console.WriteLine("2nd constructor (int + string): {0}",
                        (s + y));
}
}

// Driver Class
classGFG {

    // Main Method
    staticvoidMain()
    {

        // Creating instance and
        // passing arguments
        // It will call the first constructor
        ADD g = newADD(10, 20.2);

        // calling the method
        g.show();


        // Creating instance and
        // passing arguments
        // It will call the second constructor
        ADD q = newADD(10, "Roll No. is ");

        // calling the method
        q.show1();
    }
```

}

Output:

1st constructor (int + float): 30.2

2nd constructor (int + string): Roll No. is 10

By changing the number of the parameters

In this case, we will use two or more constructors having the different number of parameters. The data types of arguments can be the same but the number of parameters will be different.

Example:

public ADD (int a, int b);

public ADD (int a, int b, int c);

Here, the class name is **ADD**. In the first constructor the number of parameter is **two** and the types of the parameters is **int**. In second constructor the number of parameter is **three** and the types of the parameters are also **int**, their is no problem with the data types.

```
// C# Program to illustrate the overloading of
// constructor when the number of parameters
// are different
usingSystem;

classADD {

    intx, y;
    intf, p, s;

    // 1st constructor
    publicADD(inta, intb)
    {
        x = a;
        y = b;
    }

    // 2nd constructor
    publicADD(inta, intb, intc)
```

```
{
    f = a;
    p = b;
    s = c;
}

// showing 1st constructor's result
publicvoidshow()
{
    Console.WriteLine("1st constructor (int + int): {0} ",
                        (x + y));
}

// showing 2nd constructor's result
publicvoidshow1()
{
    Console.WriteLine("2nd constructor (int + int + int): {0}",
                        (f + p + s));
}
}

// Driver Class
classGFG {

    // Main Method
    staticvoidMain()
    {

        // will call 1st constructor
        ADD g = newADD(10, 20);

        // calling method
        g.show();

        // will call 2nd constructor
        ADD q = newADD(10, 20, 30);

        // calling method
        q.show1();

    }
```

}

Output:

1st constructor (int + int): 30

2nd constructor (int + int + int): 60

By changing the Order of the parameters

Example:

public student(double a, int x, string s)

public student(string s, int x, double a)

Here, the two constructor hold the same types of parameters, that is, each constructor has one **double** type, one **int** type and one **string** type parameter, but the positions of the parameters are different. The compiler will invoke the constructor according to their argument order.

```
// C# program to illustrate the overloading of
// constructor by changing the order of parameters
usingSystem;

classstudent {

    publicintroll;
    publicdoubleHeight;
    publicstringname;

    publicstudent(doublea, intx, strings)
    {
        roll = x;
        name = s;
        Height = a;
    }

    // order of the argument is different
    // with respect to 1st constructor
    publicstudent(strings, intx, doublea)
    {
        Height = a;
        roll = x;
        name = s;
```

```
    }

    publicvoidshow()
    {
        Console.WriteLine("Roll Number: "+ roll);
        Console.WriteLine("Height: "+ Height + "feet");
        Console.WriteLine("Name: "+ name);
    }
}

// Driver Class
classVaibhav {

    // Main Method
    staticvoidMain()
    {

        // invoking 1st constructor
        student s1 = newstudent(5.7, 10, "Vaibhav Singh");

        // invoking 2nd constructor
        student s2 = newstudent("Peter Perker", 11, 6.0);

        Console.WriteLine("First Constructor: ");
        s1.show();

        Console.WriteLine();

        Console.WriteLine("Second Constructor: ");
        s2.show();

    }
}
```

Output:

```
First Constructor:

Roll Number: 10

Height: 5.7feet

Name: Vaibhav Singh
```

Second Constructor:

Roll Number: 11

Height: 6feet

Name: Peter Perker

Invoke an Overloaded Constructor using "this" keyword

We can call an overloaded constructor from another constructor using **this** keyword but the constructor must be belong to the same class, because **this** keyword is pointing the members of same class in which **this** is used. This type of calling the overloaded constructor also termed as **Constructor Chaining**.

Example:

Let the class name is **gfg**,
Now
public gfg()
public gfg(int a) : this()
public gfg(double b) : this(int)

Here the first constructor is default constructor, second and third constructor are parameterized Constructor, where one has **int** type and another one has double type parameter.

In second constructor, **this()** invoke the first constructor which is *default constructor*. Here, after **this** keyword there is only ( ) which means the compiler invoke constructor that has no argument, means default constructor.

In third constructor, **this(int)** invoke the second constructor which is *parameterized constructor*. Here, after **this** there is **(int)** which means the compiler invoke constructor that has **int** type argument.

```
// C# program to illustrate the invoking of
// overloaded constructor using this keyword
usingSystem;

classGFG {

    // Private data members
    privateintLength, Height;
    privatedoubleWidth;
```

```
// Default Constructor
publicGFG()
{
    Console.WriteLine("Default Constructor Invoked");
}

// The constructor calls the
// Default constructor
publicGFG(intl, doublew) : this()
{
    Console.WriteLine("Parameterized Constructor in 2nd Constructor");

    // assigning value of
    // 'Length'and 'Width'
    Length = l;
    Width = w;

}

// The constructor call the
// parameterized constructor
publicGFG(intl, doublew, inth) : this(l, w)
{
    Console.WriteLine("Parameterized Constructor in 3rd Constructor");

    // assign value of 'Height'
    Height = h;

}

// Public Method to calculate volume
publicdoubleVolume()
{
    return(Length * Width * Height);
}
}

// Driver Class
classVaibhav {
```

```
// Main Method
publicstaticvoidMain()
{

    // Invoking 3rd Constructor
    // here Constructor chaining
    // came into existence
    GFG g = newGFG(10, 20.5, 30);

    // calling the 'Volume' Method
    Console.WriteLine("Volume is : {0}", g.Volume());

}
}
```

Output:

Default Constructor Invoked

Parameterized Constructor in 2nd Constructor

Parameterized Constructor in 3rd Constructor

Volume is : 6150

Overloading of Copy Constructor

A parameterized constructor that contains a parameter of same class type is called a copy constructor. Basically, **copy constructor** is a constructor which **copies** a data of one object into another object. Its main use is to initialize a new instance to the values of an existing instance.

```
// C# program to illustrate the
// overloading of Copy Constructor
usingSystem;

classGFG {

    publicstringp1, p2;
    publicintp3, p4;

    // 1st Constructor
    publicGFG(stringx, stringy)
    {
```

```
      p1 = x;
      p2 = y;
   }

   // Copy Constructor of 1st Constructor
   publicGFG(GFG gf)
   {
      p1 = gf.p1;
      p2 = gf.p2;
   }

   // 2nd Constructor with different
   // types pf parameter
   publicGFG(inta, intb)
   {
      p3 = a;
      p4 = b;
   }

   // Copy Constructor of 2nd Constructor
   // Here number of parameter is different
   // with respect to 1st Constructor
   publicGFG(GFG a, GFG b)
   {
      p3 = a.p3;
      p4 = b.p4;
   }
}

// Driver Class
classVaibhav {

// Main Method
staticvoidMain()
{

   // Create instance to class 'GFG'
   GFG g = newGFG(".NET Interview Questions", "By Er.Vaibhav singh Chauhan");

   // Here 'g' details will copied to 'g1'
   GFG g1 = newGFG(g);
```

```
Console.WriteLine(g1.p1 + " to "+ g1.p2);

// Create instance to class 'GFG'
// with different types of parameter
GFG G = newGFG(10, 20);

// Here 'G' details will copied to 'G1'
GFG G1 = newGFG(G, G);

Console.WriteLine("Overloaded values : {0} and {1}",
                  G1.p3, G1.p4);

}
}
```

Output:

.NET Interview Questions By Er.Vaibhav singh Chauhan

Overloaded values : 10 and 20

80.Can we overload Static Constructor?

Static Constructor cannot be overload, because Static Constructors are parameterless constructor, but for overloading, we must need parameterized constructor.

81.Can we overload private Constructor?

Private Constructor cannot be overload, because of its protection level. Private members cannot be accessed from outside the class.

82. Difference between Static Constructors and Non-Static Constructors?

Static constructors are used to initializing the static members of the class and implicitly called before the creation of the first instance of the class. Non-static constructors are used to initializing the non-static members of the class. Below are the differences between the Static Constructors and Non-Static Constructors.

- **Declaration:** Static constructors are declared using a **static modifier** explicitly while all other remaining constructors are non-static constructors. Non-static constructors can also be called as **Instance Constructors** as they need instance to get executed.

Example:

```
// C# Program to demonstrate
// how to declare the static
// constructor and non-static
// constructor
usingSystem;

class Vaibhav {
    // static variable
    staticints;

    // non-static variable
    intns;

    // declaration of
    // static constructor
    Static Vaibhav()
    {
        Console.WriteLine("It is static constructor");
    }

    // declaration of
    // non-static constructor
    Vaibhav ()
    {
        Console.WriteLine("It is non-static constructor");
    }

    // Main Method
    Static void Main(string[] args)
    {

        // static constructor will call implicitly
        // as soon as the class start to execute
        // the first block of code to execute
        // will be static constructor
```

```
        // calling non-static constructor
        Vaibhav  obj1 = new Vaibhav ();
    }
}
```

Output:

It is static constructor

It is non-static constructor

- **Calling:** Static constructors are always called implicitly but the non-static constructors are called explicitly i.e by creating the instance of the class. **Example:** In the above program, we have static constructor i.e **static Vaibhav()** which is called in the main method implicitly. See the output carefully, the code inside the static constructor is executing. But to call non-static constructor i.e **Vaibhav()**, you need to create an instance of the class, i.e *obj1*. So the creation of the object is to call the non-static constructor explicitly.

- **Execution:** Static constructor executes as soon as the execution of a class starts and it is the first block of code which runs under a class. But the non-static constructors executes only after the creation of the instance of the class. Each and every time the instance of the class is created, it will call the non-static constructor.

Example:

```
// C# Program to demonstrate
// the execution of static
// constructor and non-static
// constructor
usingSystem;

class Vaibhav {

    // declaration of
    // static constructor
    Static Vaibhav()
    {
        Console.WriteLine("Static constructor");
    }

    // declaration of
    // non-static constructor
    Vaibhav()
```

```
    {
        Console.WriteLine("Non-Static constructor");
    }

    // Main Method
    staticvoidMain(string[] args)
    {

        // static constructor will call implicitly
        // as soon as the class start to execute
        // the first block of code to execute
        // inside the class will be static
        // constructor

        // calling non-static constructor
        // here we are calling non-static
        // constructor twice as we are
        // creating two objects
        Vaibhav obj1 = new Vaibhav();
        Vaibhav obj2 = new Vaibhav();
    }
}
```

Output:

Static constructor
Non-Static constructor
Non-Static constructor

Explanation: In the above program, there are two objects of Vaibhav() class is created i.e *obj1* and *obj2*. obj1 and obj2 will call the non-static constructor twice because each and every time the instance of the class is created, it will call the non-static constructor. Although, in the Main method(entry point of a program), the first statement is *"Vaibhav obj1 = new Vaibhav();"* but as soon as the compiler found the Main Method control will transfer to class and the static block will be executed first. That's why you can see in the output that *Static Constructor* is called first.

- **Times of Execution:** A static constructor will always execute once in the entire life cycle of a class. But a non-static constructor can execute zero time if no instance of the class is created and n times if the n instances are created.

Example: In the above program, you can see the static constructor is executing only once but the non-static constructor is executing 2 times as the two instances of the class is created. If you will not create an instance of the class then the non-static constructor will not execute.

- **Initialization of fields:** Static constructors are used to initialize the static fields and non-static constructors are used to initialize the non-static fields.

Example:

```
// C# Program to demonstrate
// initialization of fields
// by using static constructor
// and non-static constructor
usingSystem;

classVaibhav {

    // static variable
    staticints;

    // non-static variable
    intns;

    // declaration of
    // static constructor
    staticVaibhav()
    {
        Console.WriteLine("Static constructor");
    }

    // declaration of
    // non-static constructor
    Vaibhav()
    {
        Console.WriteLine("Non-Static constructor");
    }

    // Main Method
    staticvoidMain(string[] args)
    {
```

```
    // static fields can
    // be accessed directly
    Console.WriteLine("Value of s is: "+ s);

    // calling non-static constructor
    Vaibhav obj1 = newVaibhav();

    // printing the value
    // of non-static field
    Console.WriteLine("Value of ns is: "+ obj1.ns);
  }
}
```

Output:

```
Static constructor

Value of s is: 0

Non-Static constructor

Value of ns is: 0
```

Explanation: Here, both the static and non-static fields are initialized with default value. The default value of int type is zero. Static constructor will initialize only static fields. Here static field is *s*. While the non-static field(*ns*) is initialized by the non-static constructor.

- **Parameters:** We cannot pass any parameters to the static constructors because these are called implicitly and for passing parameters, we have to call it explicitly which is not possible. It will give runtime error as shown in below example. However, we can pass the parameters to the non-static constructors.

Example:

```
// C# Program to demonstrate
// the passing of paramters
// to constructor
usingSystem;

classVaibhav {

    // static variable
    staticints;

    // non-static variable
    intns;
```

```
// declaration of
// static constructor
// and passing parameter
// to static constructor
staticVaibhav(intk)
{

    k = s;
    Console.WriteLine("Static constructor & K = "+ k);
}

// declaration of
// non-static constructor
Vaibhav()
{
    Console.WriteLine("Non-Static constructor");
}

// Main Method
staticvoidMain(string[] args)
{
{
}
}
}
```

Runtime Error:

prog.cs(18, 16): error CS0132: `Vaibhav.Vaibhav(int)`: The static constructor must be parameterless

- **Overloading:** Non-static constructors can be overloaded but not the static constructors. Overloading is done on the parameters criteria. So if you cannot pass the parameters to the Static constructors then we can't overload it.
- **Cases in which the constructor will be implicit:** Every class except the static class(which contains only static members) always contains an implicit constructor if the user is not defining any explicit constructor. If the class contains any static fields then the static constructors are defined implicitly.

MSQL Beginer To Intermediate

1. How to create a database in SQL?

A database is an organized file of data. It is a collection of schemas, tables, procedures, code functions, and other objects. Various query languages are used to access and manipulate data. In SQL Server, a table is the object that stores data in a tabular (columns and rows) form.

You can create a new database using CREATE DATABASE SQL command.

Syntax: CREATE DATABASE DatabaseName
Example: CREATE DATABASE Student
Or you can create a database using the SQL Server Management Studio. Right click on Databases and select New Database and follow the wizard steps.

2. What is SQL?

Structured Query Language (SQL) is a programming language for accessing and manipulating Relational Database Management Systems (RDBMSs). SQL is widely used in popular RDBMSs such as SQL Server, Oracle, and MySQL. The smallest unit of execution in SQL is a query. A SQL query is used to select, update, and delete data.

In RDBMSs, all the data is stored in tables with each table consisting of rows and columns. The following is an example of a SQL query, CREATE DATABASE.

3.What is PL/SQL?

PL/SQL (Procedural Language for SQL) is a procedural language developed by Oracle to work with Oracle database using procedures in SQL. PL/SQL program units are compiled by the Oracle Database server and stored inside the database. And at run-time, both PL/SQL and SQL run within the same server process, bringing optimal efficiency. PL/SQL automatically inherits the robustness, security, and portability of the Oracle Database. PL/SQL syntaxes includes declarations for variables, constants, procedures, functions, conditions and loops.

Control statements in PL/SQL:

- Control statements are very important in PL/SQL.
- Control Statements are elements in a program that control the flow of program execution.
- The syntax of control statements are similar to regular English and are very similar to choices that we make every day.
- Branching statements are as follows:

  o If statement
  o If - THEN - ELSE
  o Nested IF
  o Branching with logical connectivity
  o While
  o For Loop

4. What is the difference between SQL and PL/SQL?

SQL is standard query language for adding, accessing, and manipulating data in RDBMSs. SQL is a

- Only simple IF / Else statements.
- Through SQL you can interact with database through ADO.NET
- In SQL you can execute a line of code
- It can run only on windows
  PL/SQL: It is referred as Procedure Language / Structure Query Language:
- In PL/SQL you can execute a block of code not a single line of code.
- Deep control statements
- It can run in UNIX also.

- PL/SQL language includes object oriented programming techniques such as encapsulation, function overloading, and information hiding (all but inheritance).

5. What is RDBMS?

RDBMS: It is referred as Relation Database Management Systems (RDBMS).

RDBMS possesses a set of the below given characteristics:

- Write-intensive operations: The RDBMS is frequently written to and is often used in transaction-oriented applications.
- Data in flux or historical data: The RDBMS is designed to handle frequently changing data. Alternatively, RDBMS can also store vast amounts of historical data, which can later be analyzed or "mined".
- Application-specific schema: The RDBMS is configured on a per-application basis and a unique schema exists to support each application.
- Complex data models. The relational nature of the RDBMS makes it suitable for handling sophisticated, complex data models that require many tables, foreign key values, complex join operations, and so on.
- Data integrity: The RDBMS features many components designed to ensure data integrity. This includes rollback operations, referential integrity, and transaction-oriented operations.

6. What is a database table?

Database table: Table contains records in the form of rows and columns. A permanent table is created in the database you specify and remains in the database permanently, until you delete it.

Syntax:

1. **Create table** TableName (ID **INT, NAME VARCHAR**(30))
2. **Drop** syntax: **drop table** TableName
3. **Select** Syntax: **Select * from** TableName

7. How to create a table in SQL?

SQL provides an organized way for table creation:

Syntax

1. **Create table** TableName (columnName1 datatype, columnName2 dataty pe)

The following is an example of creating a simple table.

1. **create table** Info
2. (
3.   **Name varchar**(20),
4.   BirthDate **date**,
5.   Phone nvarchar(12),
6.   City **varchar**(20)
7.)

8. How to delete a table in SQL Server?

Delete Data Record from Database Table and deleting an existing table by the following method:

Syntax: To delete all table records of a table:

1. Delete TableName
2. DELETE info

9. How to update a database table using SQL?

To update an existing Table we use SQL Command UPDATE: It will update the records as per user defined query/need.

Syntax:

1. **Update** TableName **SET** ColumnName = NewData **where** Condition
2. **Update** info **Set** City = 'Baroda' **where** id = 2

10. What is a database relationship?

Relationships are created by linking the column in one table with the column in another table. There are four different types of relationship that can be created.

The relationships are listed below:

1. One to One Relationship
2. Many to One relationship
3. Many to Many relationship
4. One to One relationship

One to Many & Many to One Relationship

- For a One to many relationship, a single column value in one table has one or more dependent column values in another table. Look at the following diagram:

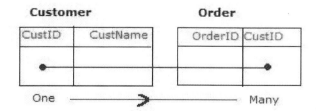

Many to Many Relationship

The third table acts as a bridge between the tables that want to establish a Many to Many relationship. The bridge table stores the common information between Many to Many relationship tables. Have a look at the following diagram:

Product			Transaction				Customer	
ProdID	ProdName		ProdID	CustID	Transdate	TotNos	CustID	CustName

11. What is a primary key of a database?

Primary key:

A table column with this constraint is called the key column for the table. This constraint helps the table to make sure that the value is not repeated and also that there are no null entries.

Now this column does not allow null values and duplicate values. You can try inserting values to violate these conditions and see what happens. A table can have only one Primary key. Multiple columns can participate on the primary key.

12. What is a foreign key of a database?

To define the relationship between two tables (one is called parent and the other one is the child table) connected by columns, a foreign key constraint is used. In this constraint the values of the child table must appear in the parent table, which means that for a foreign key, one table should point to a Primary Key in another table. A table can have multiple foreign keys and each foreign key can have a different referenced table.

Example: To understand the foreign key clearly let's assume the following two tables:

1. CUSTOMER {Cust_ID, Cust_Name, Age, ContactNo, Gender, Address}
2. VENDOR {Vend_ID, Vend_Name, Cust_ID}

Example:

Foreign Key Constraint while using CREATE TABLE statement.

Syntax

1. **CREATE TABLE** table_name
2. (
3.   Col1 datatype NOT NULL,
4.   Col2 datatype NOT NULL,
5.   Col3 datatype NOT NULL,
6.   **CONSTRAINT** FK_Column **FOREIGN KEY**(Col1, Col2, Col3) **REFERENCES** parent_table(Col1, Col2, Col3)
7.);

AT SINGLE COLUMN LEVEL

13. What is database normalization?

Database normalization is the process of organizing the fields and tables of a relational database to minimize redundancy and dependency. Normalization usually involves dividing large tables into smaller (and less redundant) tables and defining relationships among them. Normalization is a bottom-up technique for database design.

The evolution of Normalization theories is illustrated below:

- First Normal Form (1NF)
- Second Normal Form (2NF)
- Third Normal Form (3NF)
- Boyce-Codd Normal Form (BCNF)
- 4th Normal Form
- 5th Normal Form

- 6th Normal Form

14. What are database normalization forms?

Normalization is the process of organizing data into a related table. it also eliminates redundancy and increases the integrity which improves performance of the query. To normalize a database, we divide the database into tables and establish relationships between the tables.

- First Normal Form (1st NF)
- Second Normal Form (2nd NF)
- Third Normal Form (3rd NF)
- Boyce-Codd Normal Form (BCNF)
- Fourth Normal Form (4th NF)
- Fifth Normal Form (5th NF)

15. What is a stored procedure?

A Stored Procedure is a collection or a group of T-SQL statements. Stored Procedures are a precompiled set of one or more statements that are stored together in the database. They reduce the network load because of the precompilation. We can create a Stored Procedure using the "Create proc" statement.

Why we use Stored Procedure

There are several reasons to use a Stored Procedure. They are a network load reducer and decrease execution time because they are precompiled. The most important use of a Stored Procedure is for security purposes. They can restrict SQL Injection. We can avoid SQL injection by use of a Stored Procedure.

How to create a Stored Procedure

```
1. CREATE PROCEDURE spEmployee
2. AS
3. BEGIN
```

```
4.
5.  SELECT EmployeeId, Name, Gender, DepartmentName
6.  FROM tblEmployees
7.  INNER JOIN tblDepartments
8.  ON tblEmployees.EmployeeDepartmentId = tblDepartments.Departmen
    tId
9.  END
```

Advantages of using a Stored Procedure in SQL Server

- It is very easy to maintain a Stored Procedure and they are re-usable.
- The Stored Procedure retains the state of the execution plans.
- Stored Procedures can be encrypted and that also prevents SQL Injection Attacks

16. What is a function in SQL Server?

A function is a sequence of statements that accepts input, processes them to perform a specific task and provides the output. Functions must have a name but the function name can never start with a special character such as @, $, #, and so on.

Types of function

- Pre-Defined Function
- User-Defined Function

User-defined Function:

In a user-defined function we write our logic according to our needs. The main advantage of a user-defined function is that we are not just limited to pre-defined functions. We can write our own functions for our specific needs or to simplify complex SQL code. The return type of a SQL function is either a scalar value or a table.

Creation of a function

```
1.  Create function ss(@id int)
```

2. **returns table**
3. **as**
4. **return select * from** item **where** itemId = @id

Execution of a Function

1. **select * from** ss(1)

Output

17. What are the different types of functions in SQL Server?

A function must return a result. So that is also called a function that returns a result or a value. When we create it a function must specify a value type that will return a value.

- Functions only work with select statements.
- Functions can be used anywhere in SQL, such as AVG, COUNT, SUM, MIN, DATE and so on with select statements.
- Functions compile every time.
- Functions must return a value or result.
- Functions only work with input parameters.
- Try and catch statements are not used in functions.

Function Types
The following is the function list in SQL Server databases.

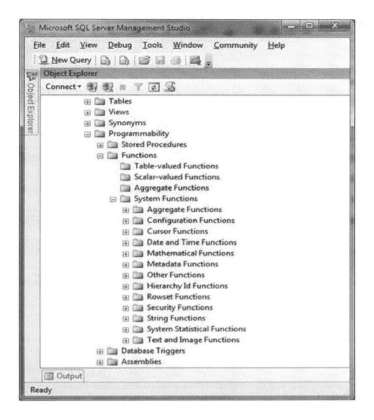

SQL Server contains the following aggregates functions:

18. What is a trigger in SQL Server?

A Trigger is a Database object just like a stored procedure or we can say it is a special kind of Stored Procedure which fires when an event occurs in a database. It is a database object that is bound to a table and is executed automatically. We cannot explicitly call any trigger. Triggers provide data integrity and used to access and check data before and after modification using DDL or DML query.

Type of Triggers

There are two types of Triggers:

1. DDL Trigger
2. DML trigger

DDL Triggers

They fire in response to DDL (Data Definition Language) command events that start with Create, Alter and Drop like Create_table, Create_view, drop_table, Drop_view and Alter_table.

Code of DDL Triggers

```
1. create trigger saftey
2. on database
3. for
4. create_table, alter_table, drop_table
5. as
6. print 'you can not create ,drop and alter table in this database'
7. rollback;
```

Output

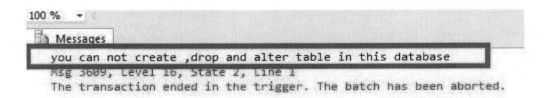

```
100 %   ▼
Messages
  you can not create ,drop and alter table in this database
  Msg 3609, Level 16, State 2, Line 1
  The transaction ended in the trigger. The batch has been aborted.
```

DML Triggers:

They fire in response to DML (Data Manipulation Language) command events that start with Insert, Update and Delete like insert_table, Update_view and Delete_table.

Code of DML Trigger:

1. **create trigger** deep
2. **on** emp
3. **for**
4. **insert, update, delete**
5. **as**
6. print 'you can notinsert,update and delete this table i'
7. **rollback**;

Output:

When we insert, update or delete in a table in a database then the following message appears:

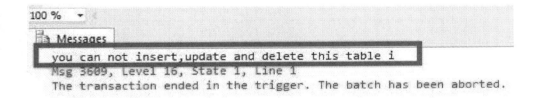

19. Why and when to use triggers?

We use a trigger when we want some event to happen automatically on certain desirable scenarios.

You have a table that changes frequently, now you want to know how many times and when these changes take place. In that case you can create a trigger that will insert the desired data into another table whenever any change in the main table occurs.

In SQL Server we can create the following 3 types of triggers:

- Data Definition Language (DDL) triggers
- Data Manipulation Language (DML) triggers
- Logon triggers

Example

```
1.  CREATE TRIGGER trgAfterInsert ON[dbo].[Employee_Test]
2.  FOR INSERT
3.  AS
4.  declare@ empid int;
5.  declare@ empname varchar(100);
6.  declare@ empsal decimal(10, 2);
7.  declare@ audit_action varchar(100);
8.  select@ empid = i.Emp_ID from inserted i;
9.  select@ empname = i.Emp_Name from inserted i;
10. select@ empsal = i.Emp_Sal from inserted i;
11. set@ audit_action = 'Inserted Record -- After Insert Trigger.';
12.
13. insert into Employee_Test_Audit
14. (Emp_ID, Emp_Name, Emp_Sal, Audit_Action, Audit_Timestamp)
15. values(@empid, @empname, @empsal, @audit_action, getdate());
16.
17. PRINT 'AFTER INSERT trigger fired.'
18. GO
```

20. What are the different types of triggers?

Triggers are a special type of stored procedure which are executed automatically based on the occurrence of a database event. These events can be categorized as:

- Data Manipulation Language (DML) and
- Data Definition Language (DDL) events.

The benefits derived from triggers is based in their events driven nature. Once created, the trigger automatically fires without user intervention based on an event in the database.

A. **Using DML Triggers:**

DML triggers are invoked when any DML command such as INSERT, DELETE, and UPDATE occurs on the data of a table and/or view.

- o DML triggers are powerful objects for maintaining database integrity and consistency.
- o DML triggers evaluate data before it has been committed to the database.
- o During this evaluation the following actions are performed.

We cannot use the following commands in DML trigger:

- o ALTER DATABASE
- o CREATE DATABASE
- o DISK DATABASE
- o LOAD DATABASE
- o RESTORE DATABASE

B. **Using DDL Triggers:**

- o These triggers focus on changes to the definition of database objects as opposed to changes to the actual data.
- o This type of trigger is useful for controlling development and production database environments.

Let us create DDL trigger now;

The following is the syntax.

1. **CREATE TRIGGER** trigger_name
2. **ON**
3. {

```
4.    ALL SERVER | DATABASE
5.  }
6.  [WITH < ddl_trigger_option > [, ...n]]
7.  {
8.    FOR | AFTER
9.  }
10. {
11.   event_type | event_group
12.   }[, ...n]
13. AS
14. {
15.   sql_statement[;][...n] | EXTERNAL NAME < method specifier > [;]

16. }
17. CREATE TRIGGER tr_TableAudit
18. ON DATABASE
19. FOR CREATE_TABLE, ALTER_TABLE, DROP_TABLE
20. AS
21. PRINT 'You must disable the TableAudit trigger in order
22. to change any table in this database '
23. ROLLBACK
24. GO
```

21. What is a view in the database?

A View is nothing but a select query with a name given to it or we can simply say a view is a Named Query. Ok! Why do we need a view? There can be many answers for this. Some of the important stuff I feel is:

1. A view can combine data from multiple tables using adequate joins and while bringing it may require complex filters and calculated data to form the required result set. From a user's point of view, all these complexities are hidden data queried from a single table.
2. Sometimes for security purposes, access to the table, table structures and table relationships are not given to the database user. All they have is access to a view not knowing what tables actually exist in the database.
3. Using the view, you can restrict the user update only portions of the records.

The following are the key points to be noted about views:

1. Multiple views can be created on one table.
2. Views can be defined as read-only or updatable.
3. Views can be indexed for better performance.
4. Insert, update, delete can be done on an updatable view.

22. What do I need views in a database?

There are a number of scenarios where we have to look for a view as a solution.

- To hide the complexity of the underlying database schema, or customize the data and schema for a set of users.
- To control access to rows and columns of data.
- To aggregate data for performance.

Views are used for security purposes because they provide encapsulation of the name of the table. Data is in the virtual table, not stored permanently. Views display only selected data.

Syntax of a View:

1. **CREATE VIEW** view_name **AS**
2. **SELECT** column_name(s)
3. **FROM** table_name
4. **WHERE** condition

There are two types of views.

- Simple View
- Complex View

23. What is an index?

An Index is one of the most powerful techniques to work with this enormous information. Database tables are not enough for getting the data efficiently in case of a huge amount of data. In order to get the data quickly we need to index the column in a table.

An index is a database object that is created and maintained by the DBMS. Indexed columns are ordered or sorted so that data searching is extremely fast. An index can be applied on a column or a view. A table can have more than one index.

Types of Index:

Microsoft SQL Server has two types of indexes. These are:

Clustered Index:

A Clustered Index sorts and stores the data in the table based on keys. A Clustered Index can be defined only once per table in the SQL Server Database, because the data rows can be sorted in only one order. Text, nText and Image data are not allowed as a Clustered index.

```
1. SET STATISTICS IO ON
2. SELECT * FROM Employee WHERE EmpID = 20001
```

EmpID	EmpName	Cell	Dept
20001	Black Smith	12345678901	1

Non-Clustered Index:

Non Clustered Indexes or simply indexes are created outside of the table. SQL Server supports 999 Non-Clustered per table and each Non-Clustered can have up to 1023 columns. A Non-Clustered Index does not support the Text, nText and Image data types.

1. **CREATE** NONCLUSTERED **INDEX** NCL_ID **ON** Employee(DeptID)

2. **SET STATISTICS** IO **ON**

1. **SELECT** * **FROM** Employee **WHERE** DeptID = 20001

EmpID	EmpName	Cell	Dept
40001	Black Smith	12345678901	20001

24. Why do I need an index in a database?

An Index is a database object that can be created on one or more columns (16 max column combinations). When creating the index it will read the column(s) and forms a relevant data structure to minimize the number of data comparisons. The index will improve the performance of data retrieval and add some overhead to the data modification such as create, delete and modify. So it depends on how much data retrieval can be done on table versus how much of DML (Insert, Delete and Update) operations.

Need of Index in Database: An index is basically used for fast data retrieval from the database.

Syntax:

1. **CREATE INDEX** index_name **ON** table_name;
2. or
3. **DROP INDEX** index_name;

Type of Index:

In a SQL Server database there are mainly the following two types of indexes:

1. Clustered index and
2. Non Clustered index

25. What is a query in a database?

SQL is a complete data manipulation language that is used not only for database queries, but also to modify and update data in the database. Compared to the complexity of the SELECT statement, which supports SQL queries, the SQL statements that modify and create database contents are somewhat simple.

However, database updates pose some challenges for a DBMS beyond those presented by database queries. The DBMS must protect the integrity of the stored data during changes, ensuring that only valid data is introduced into the database. The DBMS must also coordinate simultaneous updates by multiple users, ensuring that the users and their changes do not interfere with one another.

INSERT statement adds new rows of data to a table.

Syntax:

1. **Insert into** table_Name(**column** names) **values(Values for column)**.
2. **INSERT INTO** employee(ID, SURNAME, FIRSTNAME, EMAIL, COUNTRY, PHONE)
3. **VALUES**(111, 'vithal', 'wadje', 'vithal.wadje@yahoo.com', 'India', '+91454 5455454')

26. What are query types in a database?

Types of Commands in SQL ServerThese commands are categorized into:

* DDL
* DCL
* DML
* TCL

Let's see these categories one-by-one.

DDL

Data Definition Language (DDL) commands are the category responsible for dealing with the structure of objects. I mean that with these commands we can modify our object/entity structure. For example if there's one table and you want to modify the structure of that table, you can use DDL commands.

The following are the commands in this category:

Command   Description

Create : Used to create objects.

Alter   : Used to modify created object.

Drop : Used to delete object.

Using these commands you can create any objects like tables, views, databases, triggers, and so on.

For example:

```
1. CREATE DATABASE DB2
2. GO
3. CREATE TABLE tblDemo
4. (
5. Id int primary key,
6. Name char(20)
7. )
8. GO
9. DROP DATABASE DB2
```

DML

Data Manipulation Language (DML) commands manipulate data stored in objects like tables, views and so on. With the help these commands you can easily modify, insert and delete your data.

The following are the commands in this category:

Command Description

Insert :   Insert data into table.

Delete   :Delete data from table.

Update   : Update data into table.

Insert Into : Insert bulk data into table.

Using these commands you can manipulate any kind of data stored in entities.

For example:

```
1. INSERT INTO tblDemo VALUES(1, 'Abhishek')
2. GO
3. DELETE FROM tblDemo WHERE Id = 4
4. GO
5. UPDATE tblDemo
6. SET Name = 'Sunny'
7. WHERE Id = 6
8. GO
```

DCL

Data Control Language (DCL) commands are for security purposes. These commands are used to provide roles, permissions, access and so on.

The following are the commands in this category:
Command Description

Grant   :Provide user access to Database or any other object.

Revoke   :Take back the access from user.

For example: we have the following data.

Database: CSharpCornerDB
Table:
User: CSharpCorner

Currently we didn't provide any permission to this user.

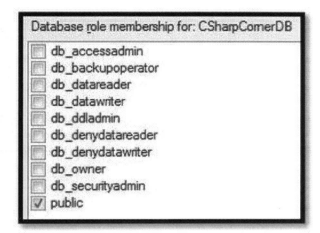

Now we'll create a table in the CSharpCornerDB database.

1. **CREATE table** tblArticles
2. (
3. ArticleId **int primary key** identity,
4. ArticleName **varchar**(10),
5. Category **varchar**(10)
6.)

If we execute this command, we'll get an error message.

Msg 262, Level 14, State 1, Line 1
CREATE TABLE permission denied in database 'CSharpCornerDB'.

This is because this user doesn't have permission to create anything right now. We'll learn how to grant or revoke permission on objects in our next article.

TCL

Transaction Control Language (TCL) commands are for managing transactions in SQL Server. The following are the commands in this category:

Command	Description
Commit	:Used to save any transaction permanently.
Rollback	:This command Is used to restore database to its last committed state.

Save Tran : This command is used to save the transaction so that we can rollback that transaction to the point whenever necessary.

For example, we have a table named "tblStudent" with 3 records as shown below:

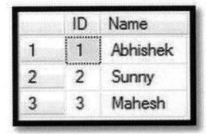

Now we'll begin our transaction and add another record and commit that transaction.

1. **Begin** Tran
2. **Insert INTO** tblStudents **VALUES**('Sumit')
3. **COMMIT**

Now we have 4 Records.

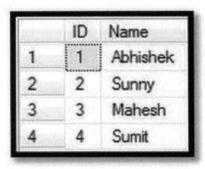

Now, we'll add three records, one by one with save point, but we don't commit our transaction.

1. **Begin** Tran
2. **Insert INTO** tblStudents **VALUES**('Kajal')
3. SAVE Tran A;
4. **Insert INTO** tblStudents **VALUES**('Rahul')
5. SAVE Tran B;
6. **Insert INTO** tblStudents **VALUES**('Ram')
7. SAVE Tran C;

8.

9. **SELECT** * **from** tblStudents

Now we have the following records in the table, from which the last three records are not yet committed.

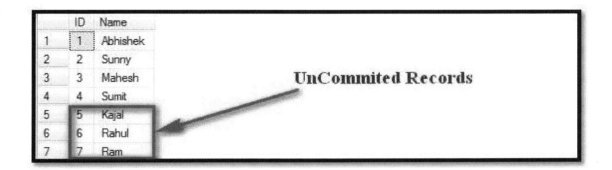

Now we have 3 savepoints, in other words A, B and C. Since our transaction is not yet committed, we can roll it back to any savepoint. We'll roll it back to point B, in other words at "Rahul".

1. ROLLBACK TRAN B
2. COMMIT Now when you fire the select query, you'll get records up to ID 6.

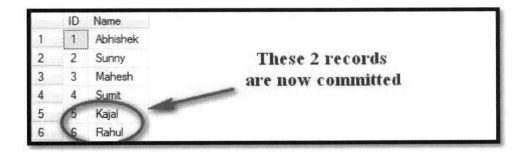

So this was the article based on types of commands in SQL Server with which you can play with data stored in SQL Server.

In this article, we have seen the types of commands in SQL Server and done some overview of that. We have also seen how to commit transactions and how to roll back any transaction to any saved point.

In my next article, we'll be explaining how to deal with the GRANT and REVOKE commands. Until then keep learning and keep sharing.

27. What is a join in SQL Server?

If You want to retrieve data from multiple tables then you need to use joins in SQL Server. Joins are used to get data from two or more tables based on the relationships among some of the columns in the tables.

Syntax

The Inner join syntax is as follows:

```
1. SELECT < column list >
2. FROM < left joined table > [INNER] JOIN < right joined table >
3. ON < join condition >
```

The example is developed in SQL Server 2012 using the SQL Server Management Studio.

Creating Table in SQL Server

Now to create 3 tables in the Master database named Table1, Table2 and Table3.

Table1

```
1. CREATE TABLE Table1
2. (
3. ID INT, Name VARCHAR(20)
4. )
```

Table2

```
1. CREATE TABLE Table2
2. (
3. ID INT, Name VARCHAR(30)
```

```
4.  )
```

Table3

```
1.  CREATE TABLE Table3
2.  (
3.  ID INT, Name VARCHAR(40)
4.  )
```

28. What are different types of joins in SQL Server?

Joins are useful for bringing data together from different tables based on their database relations. First we will see how the join operates between tables. Then we will explore the Order of Execution when both a join and a where condition exist. Finally we will move our exploration to the importance of the Join order.

A Join condition defines a way two tables are related in a query by :

- Specifying the column to be used for the Join from each table. In joining foreign keys in a table and its associated key in the other table.
- To use the logical operator in comparing values from the columns.

There are three type of joins available based on the way we join columns of two different tables.

1. Full Join
2. Inner Join
3. Left outer Join
4. Right outer Join

Full Join

A full join is somewhat different from the Cartesian product. A Cartesian product will get all the possible row combinations of the two joining tables. A Full Join takes the matching columns plus all table rows from the left table that does not match the right and all table rows in the right that does not match the left. It applies null for unmatched rows on the other end when doing so. The following example shows the full join between Table_A and Table_C

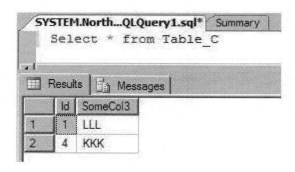

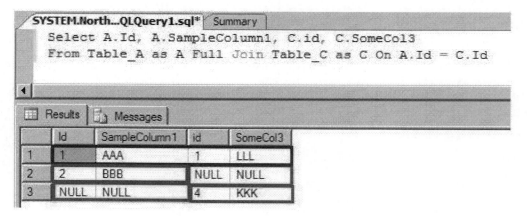

29. What is an inner join in SQL?

Inner or Self Join: This Join returns a row when there is at least one match in both tables.

let's see an example:

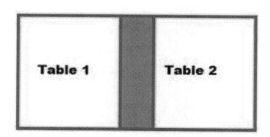

1. **Select * From** Table1
2. **Inner** Join Table2
3. **on** table1.ID = table2.ID

The following query displays the Employee Name and the corresponding Manager Name within the employee table.

1. **SELECT** e1.Employee_Name EmployeeName, e2.Employee_Name ManagerName
2. **FROM** employee e1(nolock), employee e2(nolock)
3. **WHERE** e1.EmployeeID = e2.ManagerID

Output

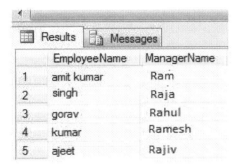

An inner join (sometimes called a "simple join") is a join of two or more tables that returns only those rows that satisfy the join condition.

30. What is an outer join in SQL?

There are three different types of outer joins; let's see 1 by 1.

- Left Outer Join
- Right Outer Join
- Full Outer Join

Left Outer Join

A LEFT OUTER JOIN is one of the JOIN operations that allows you to specify a join clause. It preserves the unmatched rows from the first (left) table, joining them with a NULL row in the shape of the second (right) table.

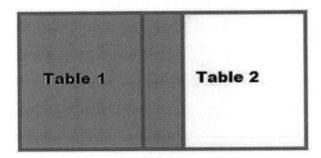

1. **Select * From** Table1
2. Left Outer Join
3. **on** table1.ID = table2.ID

Right Outer Join

A RIGHT OUTER JOIN is one of the JOIN operations that allows you to specify a JOIN clause. It preserves the unmatched rows from the Table2 (right) table, joining them with a NULL in the shape of the Table1 (left) table. A LEFT OUTER JOIN B is equivalent to B RIGHT OUTER JOIN A, with the columns in a different order.

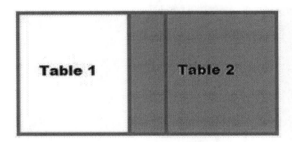

1. **Select * From** Table1
2. Right Outer Join
3. **on** table1.ID = table2.ID

31. What is full join in SQL?

A Full Outer Join fetches all records of both tables; where the record does not match, it returns Null.

1. **select** e.empId, e.empName, e1.empAdd **from** emp e **full** outer join emp_a dd e1 **on** e.empId = e1.empId

Output:

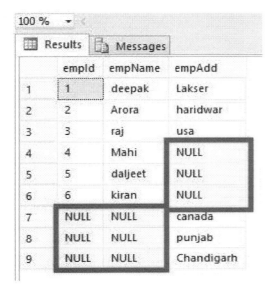

Or

Full Outer Join

FULL OUTER JOIN: This JOIN is a combination of both. All records from both Left_Table and Right_Table are in the result set and matched when they can be on the Join_Condition; when no record is found in the opposite table, NULL values are used for the columns.

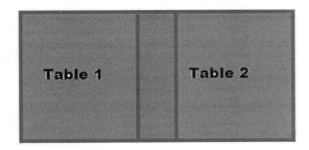

1. **Select * From** Table1
2. **Full** Outer Join
3. **on** table1.ID = table2.ID

32. What is left join in SQL Server?

Left Join: A LEFT OUTER JOIN is one of the JOIN operations that allows you to specify a join clause.

It preserves the unmatched rows from the first (left) table, joining them with a NULL row in the shape of the second (right) table.

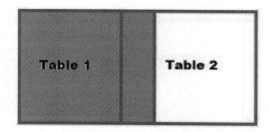

1. **Select * From** Table1
2. Left Outer Join
3. **on** table1.ID=table2.ID

A left outer join displays all the rows from the first table and the matched rows from the second table.

Example

The following query retrieves the employee name and the corresponding department he belongs to, whereas all the departments are displayed even if the employee is not assigned to any department.

1. **SELECT** e.EmployeeID, e.Employee_Name, d.Department_Name
2. **FROM** employee e(nolock) LEFT JOIN department d(nolock)
3. **ON** e.DepartmentID = d.DepartmentID

Output

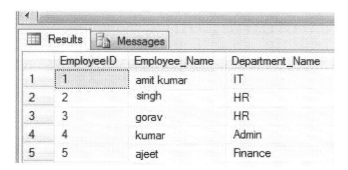

33. What is a right join in SQL Server?

Right Join: A RIGHT OUTER JOIN is one of the JOIN operations that allows you to specify a JOIN clause. It preserves the unmatched rows from the Table2 (right) table, joining them with a NULL in the shape of the Table1 (left) table. A LEFT OUTER JOIN B is equivalent to B RIGHT OUTER JOIN A, with the columns in a different order.

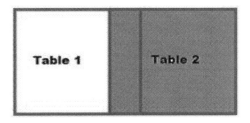

1. **Select * From** Table1
2. Right Outer Join
3. **on** table1.ID = table2.ID

The right outer join displays all the rows from the second table and matched rows from the first table.

Example

1. **SELECT** e.EmployeeID, e.Employee_Name, d.Department_Name
2. **FROM** employee e(nolock) RIGHT JOIN department d(nolock)
3. **ON** e.DepartmentID = d.DepartmentID

Output

	EmployeeID	Employee_Name	Department_Name
1	1	amit kumar	IT
2	2	singh	HR
3	3	gorav	HR
4	4	kumar	Admin
5	5	ajeet	Finance
6	NULL	NULL	Support

34. What is database engine in SQL Server?

The SQL Server Database Engine, SQL Server Agent, and several other SQL Server components run as services. These services typically are started when the operating system starts. This depends on what is specified during setup; some services are not started by default.

A service is a type of application (executable) that runs in the system background. Services usually provide core operating system features, such as Web serving, event logging, or file serving. Services can run without showing a user interface on the computer desktop. The SQL Server Database Engine, SQL Server Agent, and several other SQL Server components run as services. These services typically are started when the operating system starts. This depends on what is specified during setup; some services are not started by default.

This article describes the management of the various SQL Server services on your machine. Before you log in to an instance of SQL Server, you need to know how to start, stop, pause, resume, and restart an instance of SQL Server. After you are logged in, you can perform tasks such as administering the server or querying a database.

35. What are the Analysis Services in SQL Server?

The purpose of analysis services is to turn data into information and to provide quick and easy access to that information for decision makers. SSAS provides OLAP by letting you design, create and manage multidimensional structures that contain data aggregated from other data sources, such as relational databases and provides many data mining algorithms for mining data from data sources. So for delivering OLAP and data mining it uses client and server technologies.

The main idea of SSAS is to provide fast results from data sources when we apply a query because in order to make a decision we need data of various dimensions.
Components of the Architecture in detail.

Server Architecture: This runs as a Windows service. The Msmdsrv.exe application is a server component. This application consists of security, XMLA listener, query processor and other components that perform the following tasks:

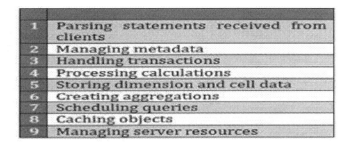

1	Parsing statements received from clients
2	Managing metadata
3	Handling transactions
4	Processing calculations
5	Storing dimension and cell data
6	Creating aggregations
7	Scheduling queries
8	Caching objects
9	Managing server resources

Client Architecture: SSAS has a thin client Component Architecture. All queries and calculations are resolved by the server only. So for each request a server to client connection is required. There are several providers with SSAS to support various programming languages. These providers communicate using SOAP packets. You can better understand this by the following diagram:

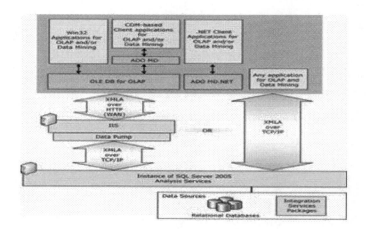

36. What are the integration services in SQL Server?

Integration Services is a platform for building high performance data integration and workflow solutions, including extraction, transformation and loading (ETL) operations for data warehousing.

This includes graphical tools and wizards for building and debugging packages.

Uses of Integration Services:

One use of Integration Services is to merge data from multiple data stores and update the data to data warehouses and/or data marts. Create the Data Transformation process logic and automate the data loading process.

Architecture of Integration Services

Architecture of Integration Services

Some important components to using Integration Services:

- SSIS Designer
- Runtime engine
- Tasks and other executables
- Data Flow engine and Data Flow components
- API or object model
- Integration Services Service

- SQL Server Import and Export Wizard
- Other tools, wizards and command prompt utilities

37. What are the data quality services in SQL Server?

SQL Server Data Quality Services:

SQL Server 2012 Data Quality Services (DQS) is the data quality product from Microsoft SQL Server 2012. DQS enables you to perform a variety of critical data quality tasks, including correction, enrichment, standardization and de-duplication of your data.

DQS provides the following features to resolve data quality issues.

- Data Cleansing
- Matching
- Reference Data Services
- Profiling and Monitoring
- Knowledge Base

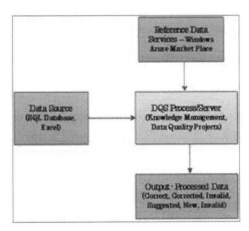

DQS enables you to perform data cleansing using cloud-based reference data services provided by reference data providers. DQS also provides profiling that is integrated into its data-quality tasks, enabling to analyze the integrity of the data.

Data Quality Server

Data Quality Server is implemented as three SQL Server catalogs DQS_MAIN, DQS_PROJECTS, and DQS_STAGING_DATA.

DQS_MAIN includes DQS Stored Procedures, DQS engine, and published Knowledge Bases.

DQS_PROJECTS includes data that is required for Knowledge Base management and DQS project activities.

DQS_STAGING_DATA provides an intermediate staging database where you can copy your source data to perform DQS operations, and then export your processed data.

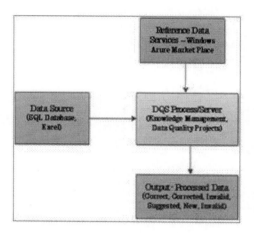

38. What are the reporting services in SQL Server?

SQL Server Reporting Services is a comprehensive reporting platform that includes processing components. Processing components are the basis for the multilayered architecture of SQL Server Reporting Services. Processing components interact with each other to retrieve data and deliver a report.

SQL Server Reporting Services has the following two basic components.

- Processors
- Extensions

Architecture of SQL Server Reporting Services

The following diagram shows the architecture of SQL Server Reporting

Services.

Architecture of SQL Server Reporting Services

Tools and Components of SQL Server Reporting Services architecture

This architecture consists mainly of the following types of components and tools.

- Report Builder
- Report Designer
- Report Manager
- Report Server
- Report server database
- Data sources

39. What are the master data services in SQL Server?

The goal of MDS is to address the challenges of both operational and analytical master data management by providing a master data hub to centrally organize, maintain, and manage your master data. This master data hub supports these capabilities with a scalable and extensible infrastructure built on SQL Server and the Windows Communication Foundation (WCF) APIs.

Master Data Services Components

The wizard installs Master Data Services Configuration Manager, installs the files necessary to run the Master Data Services Web service, and registers assemblies. After installation, you use the Master Data Services Configuration Manager to create and configure a Master Data Services database in a SQL Server instance that you specify, create the Master Data Services Web application, and enable the Web service.

Data Stewardship

Master Data Manager is the data stewardship portal in which authorized business users can perform all activities related to master data management. At minimum, a user can use this Web application to review the data in a master data model. Users with higher permissions can make changes to the master data and its structure, define business rules, review changes to master data, and reverse changes.

Model Objects

Most activities in MDS revolve around models and the objects they contain. A model is a container for all objects that define the structure of the master data. A model contains at least one entity, which is analogous to a table in a relational database. An entity contains members, which are like the rows in a table, as shown in Figure 7-1. Members (also known as leaf members) are the master data that you are managing in MDS. Each leaf member of the entity has multiple attributes, which correspond to table columns in the analogy.

Name	Code	ProductSubCategory	ProductLine	Country
Adjustable Race	AR-5381	38	NA	US
Bearing Ball	BA-8327	38	NA	US
LL Bottom Bracket	BB-7421	5	NA	US
ML Bottom Bracket	BB-8107	5	NA	US
HL Bottom Bracket	BB-9108	5	NA	US

Master Data Maintenance

Master Data Manager is more than a place to define model objects. It also allows you to create, edit, and update leaf members and consolidated members. When you add a leaf member, you initially provide values for only the Name and Code attributes, as shown in Figure 7-4. You can also use a search button to locate and select the parent consolidated member in each hierarchy.

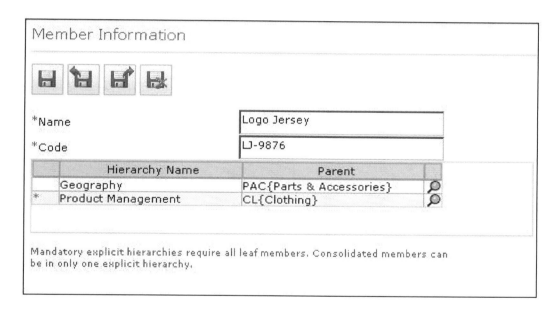

40. What is replication in SQL Server?

Replication is a process or method to synchronize the data across multiple servers. Replication is done by a replica set. A replication maintain the same data set. Replica sets provide redundancy and high availability with multiple copies of data on different database servers.

Replication removes dependencies from a single server so replication protects a database from the loss of a single server. Replication provides a mechanism to recover from hardware failure and service interruptions.

Replication is also used to increase the read capacity.

Replication provides choices for the client to select a different server for read and write operations. Replication maintains copies in different data centers to increase the locality and availability of data for distributed applications.

Example: Snapshot Replication

Step 1

Open the replication node in your database and choose the option Local Publications.

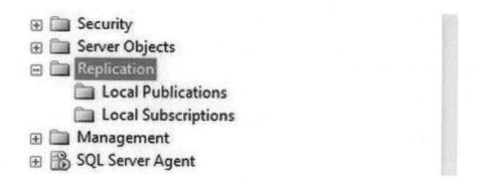

Step 2

Right-click on Local Publications and click on New publication.

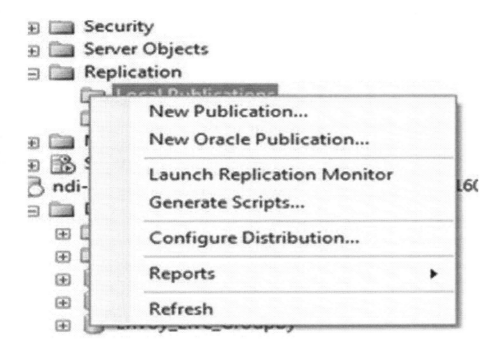

Step 3

After clicking on the new publication tab the following window will appear and click on the "Next" button.

41. How to I select data from an SQL Server table?

How to select specific rows or all columns, selecting distinct rows, filtering with where clause, sorting rows using orderby and so on.

We will be using the AdventureWorks2012 database for this demo.

1. To select all the rows and columns from a table, we use the following query:
   1. **SELECT * FROM** HumanResources.Employee

Execute the query by pressing F5 or via the execute button.

Output

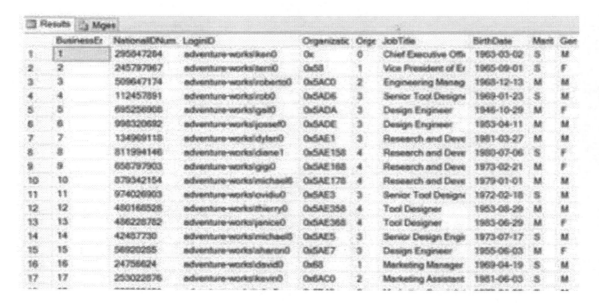

There is another way to select all the columns from a table. Instead of using *
we can specify the column names.

1. **SELECT** BusinessEntityID, NationalIDNumber, LoginID, Organization
   Node, OrganizationLevel, JobTitle, BirthDate, MaritalStatus, Gender, Hi
   reDate, SalariedFlag, VacationHours, SickLeaveHours, CurrentFlag, row
   guid, ModifiedDate **FROM** HumanResources.Employee

The output will be the same.

If you feel lazy in writing this long query given above then what you can do is
go to the Object Explorer window, then expand adventureWorks2012 then
select HumanResourcesEmployee table and right-click on it. After that "select
script table as" then select "To", then you will see a New query editor window.

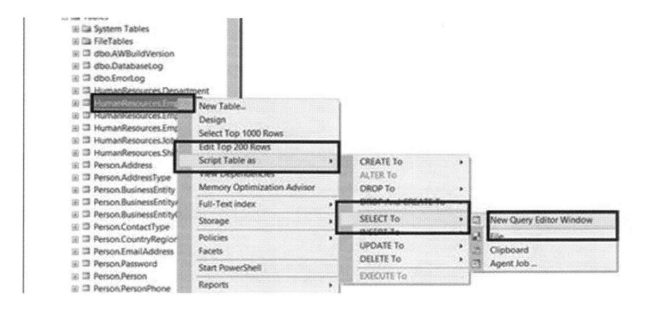

SQL Server will generate the SELECT query for us.

```
 1   USE [AdventureWorks2012]
 2   GO
 3
 4   SELECT [BusinessEntityID]
 5       ,[NationalIDNumber]
 6       ,[LoginID]
 7       ,[OrganizationNode]
 8       ,[OrganizationLevel]
 9       ,[JobTitle]
10       ,[BirthDate]
11       ,[MaritalStatus]
12       ,[Gender]
13       ,[HireDate]
14       ,[SalariedFlag]
15       ,[VacationHours]
16       ,[SickLeaveHours]
17       ,[CurrentFlag]
18       ,[rowguid]
19       ,[ModifiedDate]
20    FROM [HumanResources].[Employee]
21   GO
22
23
24
```

42. What is a check in SQL?

A Check Constraint is a rule that identifies valid values for columns of data. A Check Constraint helps to enforce Domain Integrity. If the condition in a Check Constraint is not satisfied then it prevents the value from entering into the database.

Syntax:

1. **Create table** tableName(Column1 dataType **Check**(expression), Column 2, columnN)

Example:

1. **create table** emp(empId **int check**(empId >10),empName **varchar**(15))

Output:

```
100 %    ▼
 Messages
    Command(s) completed successfully.
```

1. **insert into** emp **values**(8,'d')

Output:

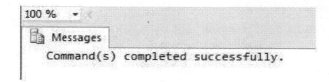

Dropping the Check Constraint:

Firstly, we can determine the name of the constraint using the following command:

1. **exec** sp_help emp

Output:

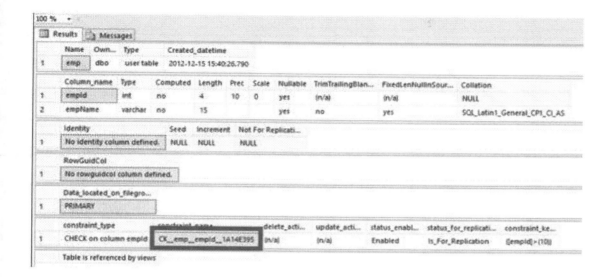

43. What is a default in SQL?

Constraints are rules that decide what kind of data can enter into the database tables. SQL server has six types of constraints and we will explore all these constraints here with suitable examples. The constraints that we are going to explore are listed below:

1. Primary Key Constraint
2. Foreign Key Constraint
3. Not Null Constraint
4. Unique constraint
5. Default Constraint
6. Check Constraint

Default Constraint

Default constraint allows you set a default value for the column. That means when a row is created for the first time, and there is no entry specified for the column that has a default constraint on it, then the default value is stored in the column.

Note that this not a Not Null constraint and do not confuse the default value constraint with disallowing the Null entries. Default value for the column is set only when the row is created for the first time and column value is ignored on the Insert. Modification to the column with NULL value or even the Insert operation specifying the Null value for the column is allowed.

Let us set the Default value of 1 for the Class. Here are the steps:

- Bring up the table designer
- Select the Class Row as you already did.
- At the bottom of the layout, you will see a Column properties as shown in the below picture. Set the default as shown below:

Column properties

44. What is a constraint in SQL?

Constraints are the rules that decide what kind of data can enter into the database tables. SQL server has six types of constraints and we will explore all these constraints here with suitable examples. The constraints that we are going to explore are listed below:

1. Primary Key Constraint
2. Foreign Key Constraint
3. Not Null Constraint
4. Unique constraint
5. Default Constraint
6. Check Constraint

First Create two tables

To explain these constraints we need two tables. Firstly, let us create these tables. Run the scripts shown below to create the tables. Copy and paste the code into the new Query Editor window, then execute it.

1. **CREATE TABLE** Student(StudId **smallint**, StudName **varchar**(50), Class tinyint);
2. **CREATE TABLE** TotalMarks(StudentId **smallint**, TotalMarks **smallint**);
3. Go

Note that there are no constraints at present on these tables. We will add the constraints one by one.

Primary Key Constraint

A table column with this constraint is called the key column for the table. This constraint helps the table to make sure that the value is not repeated and also that there are no null entries. We will mark the StudId column of the Student table as the primary key. Follow these steps:

- Right click the student table and click on the modify button
- From the displayed layout select the StudId row by clicking the Small Square like button on the left side of the row.
- Click on the Set Primary Key toolbar button to set the StudId column as primary key column.

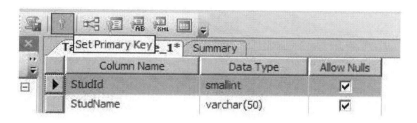

Now this column does not allow null values and duplicate values. You can try inserting values to violate these conditions and see what happens. A table can have only one Primary key. Multiple columns can participate on the primary key column. Then the uniqueness is considered among all the participant columns by combining their values.

Not Null Constraint

This constraint is useful to stop storing the null entries in the specified columns. We will mark student name column as not null column. This allows us to always having some entries in the student name column of the student table without having NULL. Follow the steps below:

- As you did previously, bring up the table design view by clicking the modify context menu for the table.
- Remove the check mark as shown in the picture below. This action will enable the Not Null constraint for the StudName column.

Table - dbo.Student1*	SYSTEM.Sample...QLQuery3.sql*	
Column Name	Data Type	Allow Nulls
StudId	smallint	☐
StudName	varchar(50)	☑
Class	tinyint	☑
		☐

Default Constraint

Default constraint allows you set a default value for the column. That means when a row is created for the first time, and there is no entry specified for the column that has a default constraint on it, then the default value is stored in the column. Note that this not a Not Null constraint and do not confuse the default value constraint with disallowing the Null entries. Default value for the column is set only when the row is created for the first time and column value is ignored on the Insert. Modification to the column with NULL value or even the Insert operation specifying the Null value for the column is allowed.

Let us set the Default value of 1 for the Class. Here are the steps:

- Bring up the table designer
- Select the Class Row as you already did.
- At the bottom of the layout, you will see a Column properties as shown in the below picture. Set the default as shown below:

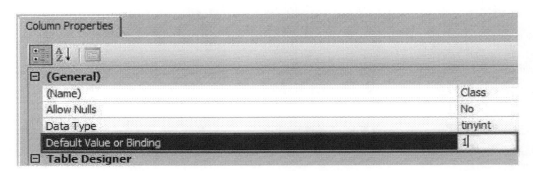

45. How do I define constraints in SQL?

Constraints

Constraints are rules and restrictions applied on a column or a table such that unwanted data can't be inserted into tables. This ensures the accuracy and reliability of the data in the database. We can create constraints on single or multiple columns of any table. Constraints maintain the data integrity and accuracy in the table.

Constraints can be classified into the following two types.

Column Types Constraints

Definitions of these types of constraints is given when the table is created.

```
1. Create Table My_Constraint
2. (
3. IID int NOT NULL,
4. Salary int CHECK(Salary > 5000)
5. )
```

Table Types Constraints

Definitions of these types of constraints is given after the creation of the table using the Alter Command.

```
1.
    1. Alter Table My_Cosntraint
2.
    1. Add constraint Check_Constraint Check(Age>50)
```

SQL Server contains the following six types of constraints:

- Not Null Constraint
- Check Constraint
- Default Constraint
- Unique Constraint
- Primary Constraint
- Foreign Constraint

Let us understand each constraint briefly.

Not Null Constraint

A Not Null constraint restrict the insertion of null values into a column. If we are using a Not Null Constraint for a column then we cannot ignore the value of this column during an insertion of data into the table.

Column Level

Syntax

```
1. CREATE TABLE Table_Name
2. (
3. Column_Name Datatype CONSTRAINT Constraint_Name NOT NULL
   ,
4. );
```

Example

```
1. Create Table My_Constraint
2. (
3. IID int NOT NULL,
4. Name nvarchar(50) CONSTRAINT Cons_NotNull not null,
5. Age int Not Null,
6. )
```

Table Level

Syntax

```
1. ALTER TABLE Table_Name
2. ALTER COLUMN Column_Name Datatype NOT NULL
```

Example

```
1. Alter Table My_Constraint
2. Alter Column IId int Not Null
```

Without SQL Command

We can also create a Not Null constraint in Microsoft SQL Server without execution of a SQL query.

First right-click on the table and select and click on the design option. Now check all the columns in the "Allow Nulls" option that should have a Null Value.

Column Name	Data Type	Allow Nulls
IID	int	☐
Salary	int	☑
Age	int	☑
		☐

Check Constraint

A Check constraint checks for a specific condition before inserting data into a table. If the data passes all the Check constraints then the data will be inserted into the table otherwise the data for insertion will be discarded. The CHECK constraint ensures that all values in a column satisfies certain conditions.

46. What is the meaning of Not Null in SQL?

Constraints are rules that decide what kind of data can enter into the database tables. SQL server has six types of constraints and we will explore all these constraints here with suitable examples. The constraints that we are going to explore are listed below:

- Primary Key Constraint
- Foreign Key Constraint
- Not Null Constraint
- Unique constraint
- Default Constraint
- Check Constraint

This constraint is useful to stop storing the null entries in the specified columns. We will mark student name column as not null column. This allows us to always have some entries in the student name column of the student table without having NULL. Here are the steps:

1. As you did previously, bring up the table design view by clicking the modify context menu for the table.
2. Remove the check mark as shown in the picture below. This action will enable the Not Null constraint for the StudName column.

Example:

Table - dbo.Student1*	SYSTEM.Sample...QLQuery3.sql*	
Column Name	Data Type	Allow Nulls
StudId	smallint	☐
StudName	varchar(50)	☑
Class	tinyint	☑
		☐

Click on the following link to read further: Table Constraints in SQL 2005

47. How to alter a table schema in SQL Server?

Altering Tables: It is used to modify an existing table.

```
1. CREATE TABLE Stock
2. (
3. ID SMALLINT
4. );
5. mysql > ALTER TABLE Stock -
        > ADD COLUMN Quantity SMALLINT UNSIGNED NOT NULL, -
        > MODIFY ID SMALLINT UNSIGNED NOT NULL, -
        > ADD PRIMARY KEY(ID);
6. mysql > Describe Stock;
7. mysql > ALTER TABLE Stock;
```

Example in Sql :

```
SET QUOTED_IDENTIFIER ON
GO

SET ANSI_PADDING ON
GO

CREATE TABLE [dbo].[Trainee1](
    [S_No] [int] NULL,
    [ID] [varchar](30) NULL,
    [Name] [char](25) NULL,
    [Age] [int] NULL,
    [City] [char](20) NULL,
    [Qualification] [varchar](20) NULL,
    [Contact_No] [varchar](30) NULL,
    [Country] [char](20) NULL,
UNIQUE NONCLUSTERED
(
    [ID] ASC
)WITH (PAD_INDEX = OFF, STATISTICS_NORECOMPUTE = OFF, IGNORE_DUP_KEY = OFF, ALLOW_ROW_LOCKS
) ON [PRIMARY]

GO

SET ANSI_PADDING OFF
GO

select * from Trainee1
alter table Trainee1 drop Column country
```

48. What are the two authentication modes in SQL Server?

There are two authentication modes –

- Windows Mode
- Mixed Mode

Modes can be changed by selecting the tools menu of SQL Server configuration properties and choose security page.

49. What Is SQL Profiler?

SQL Profiler is a tool which allows system administrator to monitor events in the SQL server. This is mainly used to capture and save data about each event of a file or a table for analysis.

50. What is recursive stored procedure?

SQL Server supports recursive stored procedure which calls by itself. Recursive stored procedure can be defined as a method of problem solving wherein the solution is arrived repetitively. It can nest up to 32 levels.

```
CREATE PROCEDURE [dbo].[Fact]
(
@Number Integer,
@RetVal Integer OUTPUT
)
AS
DECLARE @In Integer
DECLARE @Out Integer
IF @Number != 1
BEGIN
SELECT @In = @Number - 1
EXEC Fact @In, @Out OUTPUT - Same stored procedure has been called aga in(Recursively)
SELECT @RetVal = @Number * @Out
END
ELSE
BEGIN
SELECT @RetVal = 1
END
RETURN
GO
```

51. What are the differences between local and global temporary tables?

- Local temporary tables are visible when there is a connection, and are deleted when the connection is closed.

CREATE TABLE #<tablename>

- Global temporary tables are visible to all users, and are deleted when the connection that created it is closed.

CREATE TABLE ##<tablename>

52. Can SQL servers be linked to other servers?

SQL server can be connected to any database which has OLE-DB provider to give a link. Example: Oracle has OLE-DB provider which has link to connect with the SQL server group.

53. What is sub query and its properties?

A sub-query is a query which can be nested inside a main query like Select, Update, Insert or Delete statements. This can be used when expression is allowed. Properties of sub query can be defined as

- A sub query should not have order by clause
- A sub query should be placed in the right hand side of the comparison operator of the main query
- A sub query should be enclosed in parenthesis because it needs to be executed first before the main query
- More than one sub query can be included

54. What are the types of sub query?

There are three types of sub query –

- Single row sub query which returns only one row
- Multiple row sub query which returns multiple rows
- Multiple column sub query which returns multiple columns to the main query. With that sub query result, Main query will be executed.

55. What is SQL server agent?

The SQL Server agent plays a vital role in day to day tasks of SQL server administrator(DBA). Server agent's purpose is to implement the tasks easily with the scheduler engine which allows our jobs to run at scheduled date and time.

56. What are scheduled tasks in SQL Server?

Scheduled tasks or jobs are used to automate processes that can be run on a scheduled time at a regular interval. This scheduling of tasks helps to reduce human intervention during night time and feed can be done at a particular time. User can also order the tasks in which it has to be generated.

57. What is COALESCE in SQL Server?

COALESCE is used to return first non-null expression within the arguments. This function is used to return a non-null from more than one column in the arguments.

Example –

Select COALESCE(empno, empname, salary) from employee;

58. How exceptions can be handled in SQL Server Programming?

Exceptions are handled using TRY----CATCH constructs and it is handles by writing scripts inside the TRY block and error handling in the CATCH block.

59. What is the purpose of FLOOR function?

FLOOR function is used to round up a non-integer value to the previous least integer. Example is given

FLOOR(6.7)

Returns 6.

60. Can we check locks in database? If so, how can we do this lock check?

Yes, we can check locks in the database. It can be achieved by using in-built stored procedure called sp_lock.

61. What is the use of SIGN function?

SIGN function is used to determine whether the number specified is Positive, Negative and Zero. This will return +1,-1 or 0.

Example –

SIGN(-35) returns -1

62. What is an IDENTITY column in insert statements?

IDENTITY column is used in table columns to make that column as Auto incremental number or a surrogate key.

63. What is Bulkcopy in SQL?

Bulkcopy is a tool used to copy large amount of data from Tables. This tool is used to load large amount of data in SQL Server.

64. What will be query used to get the list of triggers in a database?

Query to get the list of triggers in database-

Select * from sys.objects where type='tr'

65. What is the difference between UNION and UNION ALL?

- UNION: To select related information from two tables UNION command is used. It is similar to JOIN command.
- UNION All: The UNION ALL command is equal to the UNION command, except that UNION ALL selects all values. It will not remove duplicate rows, instead it will retrieve all rows from all tables.

66. How Global temporary tables are represented and its scope?

Global temporary tables are represented with ## before the table name. Scope will be the outside the session whereas local temporary tables are inside the session. Session ID can be found using @@SPID.

67. What are the differences between Stored Procedure and the dynamic SQL?

Stored Procedure is a set of statements which is stored in a compiled form. Dynamic SQL is a set of statements that dynamically constructed at runtime and it will not be stored in a Database and it simply execute during run time.

68. What is Collation?

Collation is defined to specify the sort order in a table. There are three types of sort order –

1. Case sensitive
2. Case Insensitive
3. Binary

69. How can we get count of the number of records in a table?

Following are the queries can be used to get the count of records in a table -

Select * from <tablename> Select count(*) from <tablename> Select rows from sysindexes where id=OBJECT_ID(tablename) and indid<2

70. What is the command used to get the version of SQL Server?

Select SERVERPROPERTY('productversion')

is used to get the version of SQL Server.

71. What is UPDATE_STATISTICS command?

UPDATE_STATISTICS command is used to update the indexes on the tables when there is a large amount of deletions or modifications or bulk copy occurred in indexes.

72. What is the use of SET NOCOUNT ON/OFF statement?

By default, NOCOUNT is set to OFF and it returns number of records got affected whenever the command is getting executed. If the user doesn't want to display the number of records affected, it can be explicitly set to ON- (SET NOCOUNT ON).

73. Which SQL server table is used to hold the stored procedure scripts?

Sys.SQL_Modules is a SQL Server table used to store the script of stored procedure. Name of the stored procedure is saved in the table called Sys.Procedures.

74. What are Magic Tables in SQL Server?

During DML operations like Insert, Delete, and Update SQL Server create magic tables to hold the values during the DML operations. These magic tables are used inside the triggers for data transaction.

75. What is the difference between SUBSTR and CHARINDEX in the SQL Server?

The SUBSTR function is used to return specific portion of string in a given string. But, CHARINDEX function gives character position in a given specified string.

SUBSTRING('Smiley',1,3)

Gives result as Smi

CHARINDEX('i', 'Smiley',1)

Gives 3 as result as I appears in 3rd position of the string

76. What is the use of =,==,=== operators?

= is used to assign one value or variable to another variable. == is used for comparing two strings or numbers. === is used to compare only string with the string and number with numbers.

77. What is ISNULL() operator?

ISNULL function is used to check whether value given is NULL or not NULL in sql server. This function also provides to replace a value with the NULL.

78. What is the use of FOR Clause?

FOR clause is mainly used for XML and browser options. This clause is mainly used to display the query results in XML format or in browser.

79. What will be the maximum number of index per table?

For SQL Server 2008 100 Index can be used as maximum number per table. 1 Clustered Index and 999 Non-clustered indexes per table can be used in SQL Server.

1000 Index can be used as maximum number per table. 1 Clustered Index and 999 Non-clustered indexes per table can be used in SQL Server.

1 Clustered Index and 999 Non-clustered indexes per table can be used in SQL Server.

80. What is the difference between COMMIT and ROLLBACK?

Every statement between BEGIN and COMMIT becomes persistent to database when the COMMIT is executed. Every statement between BEGIN and ROOLBACK are reverted to the state when the ROLLBACK was executed.

81. What is the difference between varchar and nvarchar types?

Varchar and nvarchar are same but the only difference is that nvarhcar can be used to store Unicode characters for multiple languages and it also takes more space when compared with varchar.

82. What is the use of @@SPID?

A @@SPID returns the session ID of the current user process.

83. What is the command used to Recompile the stored procedure at run time?

Stored Procedure can be executed with the help of keyword called RECOMPILE.

Example

Exe <SPName> WITH RECOMPILE

Or we can include WITHRECOMPILE in the stored procedure itself.

84. How to delete duplicate rows in SQL Server?

Duplicate rows can be deleted using CTE and ROW NUMER feature of SQL Server.

85. Where are SQL Server user names and passwords stored in SQL Server?

User Names and Passwords are stored in sys.server_principals and sys.sql_logins. But passwords are not stored in normal text.

86. What is the difference between GETDATE and SYSDATETIME?

Both are same but GETDATE can give time till milliseconds and SYSDATETIME can give precision till nanoseconds. SYSDATE TIME is more accurate than GETDATE.

87. How data can be copied from one table to another table?

INSERT INTO SELECT

This command is used to insert data into a table which is already created.

SELECT INTO

This command is used to create a new table and its structure and data can be copied from existing table.

88. What is TABLESAMPLE?

TABLESAMPLE is used to extract sample of rows randomly that are all necessary for the application. The sample rows taken are based on the percentage of rows.

89. Which command is used for user defined error messages?

RAISEERROR is the command used to generate and initiates error processing for a given session. Those user defined messages are stored in sys.messages table.

90. What do mean by XML Datatype?

XML data type is used to store XML documents in the SQL Server database. Columns and variables are created and store XML instances in the database.

91. What is CDC?

CDC is abbreviated as Change Data Capture which is used to capture the data that has been changed recently. This feature is present in SQL Server 2008.

92. What is SQL injection?

SQL injection is an attack by malicious users in which malicious code can be inserted into strings that can be passed to an instance of SQL server for parsing and execution. All statements have to checked for vulnerabilities as it executes all syntactically valid queries that it receives.

Even parameters can be manipulated by the skilled and experienced attackers.

93. What are the methods used to protect against SQL injection attack?

Following are the methods used to protect against SQL injection attack:

- Use Parameters for Stored Procedures
- Filtering input parameters
- Use Parameter collection with Dynamic SQL
- In like clause, user escape characters

94. What is Filtered Index?

Filtered Index is used to filter some portion of rows in a table to improve query performance, index maintenance and reduces index storage costs. When the index is created with WHERE clause, then it is called Filtered Index

MVC

1. Explain what is Model-View-Controller?

MVC is a software architecture pattern for developing web application. It is handled by three objects Model-View-Controller.

2. Mention what does Model-View-Controller represent in an MVC application?

In an MVC model,

- **Model-** It represents the application data domain. In other words applications business logic is contained within the model and is responsible for maintaining data
- **View-** It represents the user interface, with which the end users communicates. In short all the user interface logic is contained within the VIEW
- **Controller-** It is the controller that answers to user actions. Based on the user actions, the respective controller responds within the model and choose a view to render that display the user interface. The user input logic is contained with-in the controller

3. Explain in which assembly is the MVC framework is defined?

The MVC framework is defined in System.Web.Mvc.

4. List out few different return types of a controller action method?

- View Result
- Javascript Result
- Redirect Result
- Json Result
- Content Result

5. Mention what is the difference between adding routes, to a webform application and an MVC application?

To add routes to a webform application, we can use MapPageRoute() method of the RouteCollection class, where adding routes to an MVC application, you can use MapRoute() method.

6. Mention what are the two ways to add constraints to a route?

The two methods to add constraints to a route is

- Use regular expressions
- Use an object that implements IRouteConstraint Interface

7. Mention what is the advantages of MVC?

- MVC segregates your project into a different segment, and it becomes easy for developers to work on
- It is easy to edit or change some part of your project that makes project less development and maintenance cost
- MVC makes your project more systematic

8. Mention what "beforFilter()","beforeRender" and "afterFilter" functions do in Controller?

- **beforeFilter():** This function is run before every action in the controller. It's the right place to check for an active session or inspect user permissions.
- **beforeRender():** This function is called after controller action logic, but before the view is rendered. This function is not often used, but may be required If you are calling render() manually before the end of a given action
- **afterFilter():** This function is called after every controller action, and after rendering is done. It is the last controller method to run

9. Explain the role of components Presentation, Abstraction and Control in MVC?

- **Presentation:** It is the visual representation of a specific abstraction within the application

- **Abstraction:** It is the business domain functionality within the application
- **Control:** It is a component that keeps consistency between the abstraction within the system and their presentation to the user in addition to communicating with other controls within the system

10. Mention the advantages and disadvantages of MVC model?

Advantages

It represents clear separation between business logic and presentation logic

Each MVC object has different responsibilities

The development progresses in parallel

Easy to manage and maintain

All classes and object are independent of each other

Disadvantages

The model pattern is little complex

Inefficiency of data access in view

With modern user interface, it is difficult to use MVC

You need multiple programmers for parallel development

Multiple technologies knowledge is required

11. Explain the role of "ActionFilters" in MVC?

In MVC " ActionFilters" help you to execute logic while MVC action is executed or its executing.

12. Explain what are the steps for the execution of an MVC project?

The steps for the execution of an MVC project includes

- Receive first request for the application
- Performs routing
- Creates MVC request handler
- Create Controller
- Execute Controller
- Invoke action
- Execute Result

13. Explain what is routing? What are the three segments for routing is important?

Routing helps you to decide a URL structure and map the URL with the Controller.

The three segments that are important for routing is

- ControllerName
- ActionMethodName
- Parameter

14. Explain how routing is done in MVC pattern?

There is a group of routes called the RouteCollection, which consists of registered routes in the application. The RegisterRoutes method records the routes in this collection. A route defines a URL pattern and a handler to use if the request matches the pattern. The first parameter to the MapRoute method is the name of the route. The second parameter will be the pattern to which the URL matches. The third parameter might be the default values for the placeholders if they are not determined.

15. Explain using hyperlink how you can navigate from one view to other view?

By using "ActionLink" method as shown in the below code. The below code will make a simple URL which help to navigate to the "Home" controller and invoke the "GotoHome" action.

Collapse / Copy Code

<%= Html.ActionLink("Home", "Gotohome") %>

16. Mention how can maintain session in MVC?

Session can be maintained in MVC by three ways tempdata, viewdata, and viewbag.

17. Mention what is the difference between Temp data, View, and View Bag?

- Temp data: It helps to maintain data when you shift from one controller to other controller.
- View data: It helps to maintain data when you move from controller to view
- View Bag: It's a dynamic wrapper around view data

18. What is partial view in MVC?

Partial view in MVC renders a portion of view content. It is helpful in reducing code duplication. In simple terms, partial view allows to render a view within the parent view.

19. Explain how you can implement Ajax in MVC?

In MVC, Ajax can be implemented in two ways

- Ajax libraries
- Jquery

20. Mention what is the difference between "ActionResult" and "ViewResult" ?

"ActionResult" is an abstract class while "ViewResult" is derived from "AbstractResult" class. "ActionResult" has a number of derived classes like "JsonResult", "FileStreamResult" and "ViewResult" .

"ActionResult" is best if you are deriving different types of view dynamically.

21. Explain how you can send the result back in JSON format in MVC?

In order to send the result back in JSON format in MVC, you can use "JSONRESULT" class.

22. Explain what is the difference between View and Partial View?

View

It contains the layout page

Before any view is rendered, viewstart page is rendered

View might have markup tags like body, html, head, title, meta etc.

View is not lightweight as compare to Partial View

Partial View

It does not contain the layout page

Partial view does not verify for a viewstart.cshtml. We cannot put common code for a partial view within the viewStart.cshtml.page

Partial view is designed specially to render within the view and just because of that it does not consist any mark up

We can pass a regular view to the RenderPartial method

23. List out the types of result in MVC?

In MVC, there are twelve types of results in MVC where "ActionResult" class is the main class while the 11 are their sub-types

- ViewResult
- PartialViewResult
- EmptyResult
- RedirectResult

- RedirectToRouteResult
- JsonResult
- JavaScriptResult
- ContentResult
- FileContentResult
- FileStreamResult
- FilePathResult

24. Mention what is the importance of NonActionAttribute?

All public methods of a controller class are treated as the action method if you want to prevent this default method then you have to assign the public method with NonActionAttribute.

25. Mention what is the use of the default route {resource}.axd/{*pathinfo} ?

This default route prevents request for a web resource file such as Webresource.axd or ScriptResource.axd from being passed to the controller.

26. Mention the order of the filters that get executed, if the multiple filters are implemented?

The filter order would be like

- Authorization filters
- Action filters
- Response filters
- Exception filters

27. Mention what filters are executed in the end?

In the end "Exception Filters" are executed.

28. Mention what are the file extensions for razor views?

For razor views the file extensions are

- .cshtml: If C# is the programming language
- .vbhtml: If VB is the programming language

29. Mention what are the two ways for adding constraints to a route?

Two methods for adding constraints to route is

- Using regular expressions
- Using an object that implements IRouteConstraint interface

30. Mention two instances where routing is not implemented or required?

Two instance where routing is not required are

- When a physical file is found that matches the URL pattern
- When routing is disabled for a URL pattern

31. Mention what are main benefits of using MVC?

There are two key benefits of using MVC

- As the code is moved behind a separate class file, you can use the code to a great extent
- As behind code is simply moved to.NET class, it is possible to automate UI testing. This gives an opportunity to automate manual testing and write unit tests.

32.Can you explain the page life cycle of MVC?

Below are the processed followed in the sequence –

→App initialization

→Routing

→Instantiate and execute controller

→Locate and invoke controller action

→Instantiate and render view.

33. What is Separation of Concerns in ASP.NET MVC?

It's is the process of breaking the program into various distinct features which overlaps in functionality as little as possible. MVC pattern concerns on separating the content from presentation and data-processing from content.

34. What is Razor View Engine?

Razor is the first major update to render HTML in MVC 3. Razor was designed specifically for view engine syntax. Main focus of this would be to simplify and code-focused templating for HTML generation. Below is the sample of using Razor:

@model MvcMusicStore.Models.Customer

@{ViewBag.Title = "Get Customers";}

<div class="cust"> <h3><em>@Model.CustomerName</em> </h3>

35. What is the meaning of Unobtrusive JavaScript?

This is a general term that conveys a general philosophy, similar to the term REST (Representational State Transfer). Unobtrusive JavaScript doesn't intermix JavaScript code in your page markup.

Eg : Instead of using events like onclick and onsubmit, the unobtrusive JavaScript attaches to elements by their ID or class based on the HTML5 data-attributes.

36. What is the use of ViewModel in MVC?

ViewModel is a plain class with properties, which is used to bind it to strongly typed view. ViewModel can have the validation rules defined for its properties using data annotations.

37. What are Actions in MVC?

Actions are the methods in Controller class which is responsible for returning the view or json data. Action will mainly have return type — "ActionResult" and it will be invoked from method — "InvokeAction()" called by controller.

38. What is Attribute Routing in MVC?

ASP.NET Web API supports this type routing. This is introduced in MVC5. In this type of routing, attributes are being used to define the routes. This type of routing gives more control over classic URI Routing. Attribute Routing can be defined at controller level or at Action level like –

[Route("{action = TestCategoryList}")] — Controller Level

[Route("customers/{TestCategoryId:int:min(10)}")] — Action Level

39. How to enable Attribute Routing?

Just add the method — "MapMvcAttributeRoutes()" to enable attribute routing as shown below

public static void RegistearRoutes(RouteCollection routes)

{

routes.IgnoareRoute("{resource}.axd/{*pathInfo}");

//enabling attribute routing

routes.MapMvcAttributeRoutes();

//convention-based routing

routes.MapRoute

(

name: "Default",

url: "{controller}/{action}/{id}",

defaults: new { controller = "Customer", action = "GetCustomerList", id = UrlParameter.Optional }

);

}

40. Explain JSON Binding?

JavaScript Object Notation (JSON) binding support started from MVC3 onwards via the new JsonValueProviderFactory, which allows the action methods to accept and model-bind data in JSON format. This is useful in Ajax scenarios like client templates and data binding that need to post data back to the server.

41. Explain Dependency Resolution?

Dependency Resolver again has been introduced in MVC3 and it is greatly simplified the use of dependency injection in your applications. This turn to be easier and useful for decoupling the application components and making them easier to test and more configurable.

42. Explain Bundle.Config in MVC4?

"BundleConfig.cs" in MVC4 is used to register the bundles by the bundling and minification system. Many bundles are added by default including jQuery libraries like — jquery.validate, Modernizr, and default CSS references.

43. How route table has been created in ASP.NET MVC?

Method — "RegisterRoutes()" is used for registering the routes which will be added in "Application_Start()" method of global.asax file, which is fired when the application is loaded or started.

44. Which are the important namespaces used in MVC?

Below are the important namespaces used in MVC -

System.Web.Mvc

System.Web.Mvc.Ajax

System.Web.Mvc.Html

System.Web.Mvc.Async

45. What is ViewData?

Viewdata contains the key, value pairs as dictionary and this is derived from class — "ViewDataDictionary". In action method we are setting the value for viewdata and in view the value will be fetched by typecasting.

46. What is the difference between ViewBag and ViewData in MVC?

ViewBag is a wrapper around ViewData, which allows to create dynamic properties. Advantage of viewbag over viewdata will be –

In ViewBag no need to typecast the objects as in ViewData.

ViewBag will take advantage of dynamic keyword which is introduced in version 4.0. But before using ViewBag we have to keep in mind that ViewBag is slower than ViewData.

47. Explain TempData in MVC?

TempData is again a key, value pair as ViewData. This is derived from "TempDataDictionary" class. TempData is used when the data is to be used in two consecutive requests, this could be between the actions or between the controllers. This requires typecasting in view.

48. What are HTML Helpers in MVC?

HTML Helpers are like controls in traditional web forms. But HTML helpers are more lightweight compared to web controls as it does not hold viewstate and events.

HTML Helpers returns the HTML string which can be directly rendered to HTML page. Custom HTML Helpers also can be created by overriding "HtmlHelper" class.

49. What are AJAX Helpers in MVC?

AJAX Helpers are used to create AJAX enabled elements like as Ajax enabled forms and links which performs the request asynchronously and these are extension methods of AJAXHelper class which exists in namespace — System.Web.Mvc.

50. What are the options can be configured in AJAX helpers?

Below are the options in AJAX helpers –

Url — This is the request URL.

Confirm — This is used to specify the message which is to be displayed in confirm box.

OnBegin — Javascript method name to be given here and this will be called before the AJAX request.

OnComplete — Javascript method name to be given here and this will be called at the end of AJAX request.

OnSuccess — Javascript method name to be given here and this will be called when AJAX request is successful.

OnFailure — Javascript method name to be given here and this will be called when AJAX request is failed.

UpdateTargetId — Target element which is populated from the action returning HTML.

51. What is Layout in MVC?

Layout pages are similar to master pages in traditional web forms. This is used to set the common look across multiple pages. In each child page we can find — /p>

@{

Layout = "~/Views/Shared/TestLayout1.cshtml";

}

This indicates child page uses TestLayout page as it's master page.

52. Explain Sections is MVC?

Section are the part of HTML which is to be rendered in layout page. In Layout page we will use the below syntax for rendering the HTML –

@RenderSection("TestSection")

And in child pages we are defining these sections as shown below –

@section TestSection{

<h1>Test Content</h1>

}

If any child page does not have this section defined then error will be thrown so to avoid that we can render the HTML like this –

@RenderSection("TestSection", required: false)

53. Can you explain RenderBody and RenderPage in MVC?

RenderBody is like ContentPlaceHolder in web forms. This will exist in layout page and it will render the child pages/views. Layout page will have only one RenderBody() method. RenderPage also exists in Layout page and multiple RenderPage() can be there in Layout page.

54. What is ViewStart Page in MVC?

This page is used to make sure common layout page will be used for multiple views. Code written in this file will be executed first when application is being loaded.

55. Explain the methods used to render the views in MVC?

Below are the methods used to render the views from action –

View() — To return the view from action.

PartialView() — To return the partial view from action.

RedirectToAction() — To Redirect to different action which can be in same controller or in different controller.

Redirect() — Similar to "Response.Redirect()" in webforms, used to redirect to specified URL.

RedirectToRoute() — Redirect to action from the specified URL but URL in the route table has been matched.

56. What are the sub types of ActionResult?

ActionResult is used to represent the action method result. Below are the subtypes of ActionResult –

ViewResult

PartialViewResult

RedirectToRouteResult

RedirectResult

JavascriptResult

JSONResult

FileResult

HTTPStatusCodeResult

57. What are Non Action methods in MVC?

In MVC all public methods have been treated as Actions. So if you are creating a method and if you do not want to use it as an action method then the method has to be decorated with "NonAction" attribute as shown below –

[NonAction]

public void TestMethod()

{

// Method logic

}

58. How to change the action name in MVC?

"ActionName" attribute can be used for changing the action name. Below is the sample code snippet to demonstrate more –

[ActionName("TestActionNew")]

public ActionResult TestAction()

{

return View();

}

So in the above code snippet "TestAction" is the original action name and in "ActionName" attribute, name — "TestActionNew" is given. So the caller of this action method will use the name "TestActionNew" to call this action.

59. What are Code Blocks in Views?

Unlike code expressions that are evaluated and sent to the response, it is the blocks of code that are executed. This is useful for declaring variables which we may be required to be used later.

@{

```
int x = 123;

string y = "aa";

}
```

60. What is the "HelperPage.IsAjax" Property?

The HelperPage.IsAjax property gets a value that indicates whether Ajax is being used during the request of the Web page.

61. How we can call a JavaScript function on the change of a Dropdown List in MVC?

Create a JavaScript method:

```
<script type="text/javascript">

function DrpIndexChanged() { }

</script>
```

Invoke the method:

```
<%:Html.DropDownListFor(x => x.SelectedProduct, new
SelectList(Model.Customers, "Value", "Text"), "Please Select a Customer", new {
id = "ddlCustomers", onchange=" DrpIndexChanged ()" })%>
```

62. What are Validation Annotations?

Data annotations are attributes which can be found in the "System.ComponentModel.DataAnnotations" namespace. These attributes will be used for server-side validation and client-side validation is also supported. Four attributes — Required, String Length, Regular Expression and Range are used to cover the common validation scenarios.

63. Why to use Html.Partial in MVC?

This method is used to render the specified partial view as an HTML string. This method does not depend on any action methods. We can use this like below —

@Html.Partial("TestPartialView")

64. What is Html.RenderPartial?

Result of the method — "RenderPartial" is directly written to the HTML response. This method does not return anything (void). This method also does not depend on action methods. RenderPartial() method calls "Write()" internally and we have to make sure that "RenderPartial" method is enclosed in the bracket. Below is the sample code snippet –
@{Html.RenderPartial("TestPartialView"); }

65. What is RouteConfig.cs in MVC ?

"RouteConfig.cs" holds the routing configuration for MVC. RouteConfig will be initialized on Application_Start event registered in Global.asax.

66. What are Scaffold templates in MVC?

Scaffolding in ASP.NET MVC is used to generate the Controllers,Model and Views for create, read, update, and delete (CRUD) functionality in an application.

The scaffolding will be knowing the naming conventions used for models and controllers and views.

67. Explain the types of Scaffoldings.

Below are the types of scaffoldings –

Empty

Create

Delete

Details

Edit

List

68. Can a view be shared across multiple controllers? If Yes, How we can do that?

Yes, we can share a view across multiple controllers. We can put the view in the "Shared" folder. When we create a new MVC Project we can see the Layout page will be added in the shared folder, which is because it is used by multiple child pages.

69. What are the components required to create a route in MVC?

Name — This is the name of the route.

URL Pattern — Placeholders will be given to match the request URL pattern.

Defaults —When loading the application which controller, action to be loaded along with the parameter.

70. What is PartialView in MVC?

PartialView is similar to UserControls in traditional web forms. For re-usability purpose partial views are used. Since it's been shared with multiple views these are kept in shared folder. Partial Views can be rendered in following ways —

Html.Partial()

Html.RenderPartial()

71. How we can add the CSS in MVC?

Below is the sample code snippet to add css to razor views —

<link rel="StyleSheet" href="/@Href(~Content/Site.css")" type="text/css"/>

72. Can I add MVC Testcases in Visual Studio Express?

No. We cannot add the test cases in Visual Studio Express edition it can be added only in Professional and Ultimate versions of Visual Studio.

73. What is the use .Glimpse in MVC?

Glimpse is an open source tool for debugging the routes in MVC. It is the client side debugger. Glimpse has to be turned on by visiting to local url link -

http://localhost:portname//glimpse.axd

This is a popular and useful tool for debugging which tracks the speed details, url details etc.

74. What are Filters in MVC?

In MVC, controllers define action methods and these action methods generally have a one-to-one relationship with UI controls such as clicking a button or a link, etc. For example, in one of our previous examples, the UserController class contained methods UserAdd, UserDelete, etc.

But many times we would like to perform some action before or after a particular operation. For achieving this functionality, ASP.NET MVC provides feature to add pre and post action behaviors on controller's action methods.

Types of Filters

ASP.NET MVC framework supports the following action filters,

- *Action Filters*
  Action filters are used to implement logic that gets executed before and after a controller action executes. We will look at Action Filters in detail in this chapter.

- *Authorization Filters*
  Authorization filters are used to implement authentication and authorization for controller actions.

- *Result Filters*
  Result filters contain logic that is executed before and after a view result is executed. For example, you might want to modify a view result right

before the view is rendered to the browser.

- *Exception Filters*
  Exception filters are the last type of filter to run. You can use an exception filter to handle errors raised by either your controller actions or controller action results. You can also use exception filters to log errors.

Action filters are one of most commonly used filters to perform additional data processing, or manipulating the return values or cancelling the execution of action or modifying the view structure at run time.

75.Differences between Razor and ASPX View Engine in MVC?

Razor View Engine	ASPX View Engine (Web form view engine)
The namespace used by the Razor View Engine is System.Web.Razor	The namespace used by the ASPX View Engine is System.Web.Mvc.WebFormViewEngine
The file extensions used by the Razor View Engine are different from a web form view engine. It uses cshtml with C# and vbhtml with vb for views, partial view, templates and layout pages.	The file extensions used by the Web Form View Engines are like ASP.Net web forms. It uses the ASPX extension to view the aspc extension for partial views or User Controls or templates and master extensions for layout/master pages.
The Razor View Engine is an advanced view engine that was introduced with MVC 3.0. This is not a new language but it is markup.	A web form view engine is the default view engine and available from the beginning of MVC
Razor has a syntax that is very compact and helps us	The web form view engine has syntax that is the

to reduce typing.	same as an ASP.Net forms application.
The Razor View Engine uses @ to render server-side content.	The ASPX/web form view engine uses "<%= %>" or "<%: %>" to render server-side content.
By default all text from an @ expression is HTML encoded.	There is a different syntax ("<%: %>") to make text HTML encoded.
Razor does not require the code block to be closed, the Razor View Engine parses itself and it is able to decide at runtime which is a content element and which is a code element.	A web form view engine requires the code block to be closed properly otherwise it throws a runtime exception.
The Razor View Engine prevents Cross Site Scripting (XSS) attacks by encoding the script or HTML tags before rendering to the view.	A web form View engine does not prevent Cross Site Scripting (XSS) attack.
The Razor Engine supports Test Driven Development (TDD).	Web Form view engine does not support Test Driven Development (TDD) because it depends on the System.Web.UI.Page class to make the testing complex.
Razor uses "@* â€¦ *@" for multiline comments.	The ASPX View Engine uses "<!--...-->" for markup and "/* â€¦ */" for C# code.
There is only three transition characters with the Razor View Engine.	There are only three transition characters with the Razor View Engine.

The Razor View Engine is a bit slower than the ASPX View Engine.

Conclusion

Razor provides a new view engine with streamlined code for focused templating. Razor's syntax is very compact and improves readability of the markup and code. By default MVC supports ASPX (web forms) and Razor View Engine. MVC also supports third-party view engines like Spark, Nhaml, NDjango, SharpDOM and so on. ASP.NET MVC is open source.

76. What are the Main Razor Syntax Rules?

- Razor code blocks are enclosed in @{ ... }
- Inline expressions (variables and functions) start with @
- Code statements end with semicolon
- Variables are declared with the var keyword
- Strings are enclosed with quotation marks
- C# code is case sensitive
- C# files have the extension .cshtml

C# Example

```
1.  <!-- Single statement block -->
2.  @ {
3.      varmyMessage = "Hello World";
4.  }
5.  <!-- Inline expression or variable -->
6.  < p > The value of myMessage is: @myMessage < /p>
7.      <!-- Multi-statement block -->
8.  @ {
9.      var greeting = "Welcome to our site!";
10.     varweekDay = DateTime.Now.DayOfWeek;
11.     vargreetingMessage = greeting + " Here in Huston it is: " + weekDay;

12. } < p > The greeting is: @greetingMessage < /p>
```

77.How do you implement Forms authentication in MVC?

Authentication is giving access to the user for a specific service by verifying his/her identity using his/her credentials like username and password or email and password. It assures that the correct user is authenticated or logged in for a specific service and the right service has been provided to the specific user based on their role that is nothing but authorization.

ASP.NET forms authentication occurs after IIS authentication is completed. You can configure forms authentication by using forms element with in web.config file of your application. The default attribute values for forms authentication are shown below,

```
1.  <system.web>
2.    <authenticationmode="Forms">
3.      <formsloginUrl="Login.aspx" protection="All" timeout="30" name
    =".ASPXAUTH" path="/" requireSSL="false" slidingExpiration="true"
     defaultUrl="default.aspx" cookieless="UseDeviceProfile" enableCrossA
     ppRedirects="false" />
4.      </authentication>
5.  </system.web>
```

The FormsAuthentication class creates the authentication cookie automatically when SetAuthCookie() or RedirectFromLoginPage() methods are called. The value of authentication cookie contains a string representation of the encrypted and signed FormsAuthenticationTicket object.

78.Explain Areas in MVC?

From ASP.Net MVC 2.0 Microsoft provided a new feature in MVC applications, Areas. Areas are just a way to divide or "isolate" the modules of large applications in multiple or separated MVC. like,

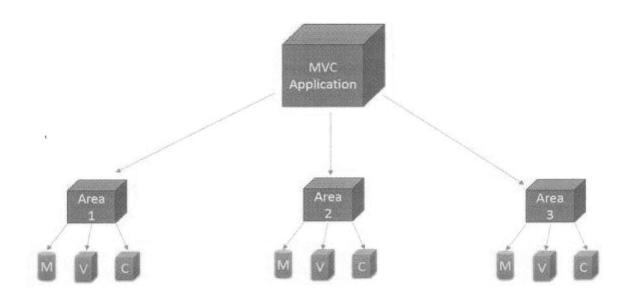

When you add an area to a project, a route for the area is defined in an AreaRegistration file. The route sends requests to the area based on the request URL. To register routes for areas, you add code to theGlobal.asax file that can automatically find the area routes in the AreaRegistration file.

AreaRegistration.RegisterAllAreas();

Benefits of Area in MVC

1. Allows us to organize models, views and controllers into separate functional sections of the application, such as administration, billing, customer support and much more.
2. Easy to integrate with other Areas created by another.
3. Easy for unit testing.

79.Explain the need of display mode in MVC?

DisplayModes give you another level of flexibility on top of the default capabilities we saw in the last section. DisplayModes can also be used along with the previous feature so we will simply build off of the site we just created.

Using display modes involves in 2 steps

1. We should register Display Mode with a suffix for particular browser using "DefaultDisplayMode"e class inApplication_Start() method in the Global.asax file.
2. View name for particular browser should be appended with suffix mentioned in first step.

1. Desktop browsers (without any suffix. e.g.: Index.cshtml, _Layout.cshtml).
2. Mobile browsers (with a suffix "Mobile". e.g.: Index.Mobile.cshtml,Layout.Mobile.cshtml)
   If you want design different pages for different mobile device browsers (any different browsers) and render them depending on the browser requesting. To handle these requests you can register custom display modes. We can do that using DisplayModeProvider.Instance.Modes.Insert(int index, IDisplayMode item) method.

80. What is Output Caching in MVC?

The main purpose of using Output Caching is to dramatically improve the performance of an ASP.NET MVC Application. It enables us to cache the content returned by any controller method so that the same content does not need to be generated each time the same controller method is invoked. Output Caching has huge advantages, such as it reduces server round trips, reduces database server round trips, reduces network traffic etc.

Keep the following in mind,

- Avoid caching contents that are unique per user.
- Avoid caching contents that are accessed rarely.
- Use caching for contents that are accessed frequently.

Let's take an example. My MVC application displays a list of database records on the view page so by default each time the user invokes the controller method to see records, the application loops through the entire process and executes the database query. And this can actually decrease the application performance. So, we can advantage of the "Output Caching" that avoids executing database queries each time the user invokes the controller method. Here the view page is retrieved from the cache instead of invoking the controller method and doing redundant work.

Cached Content Locations

In the above paragraph I said, in Output Caching the view page is retrieved from the cache, so where is the content cached/stored?

Please note, there is no guarantee that content will be cached for the amount of time that we specify. When memory resources become low, the cache starts evicting content automatically.

OutputCache label has a "Location" attribute and it is fully controllable. Its default value is "Any", however there are the following locations available; as of now, we can use any one.

1. Any
2. Client
3. Downstream
4. Server
5. None
6. ServerAndClient

With "Any", the output cache is stored on the server where the request was processed. The recommended store cache is always on the server very carefully. You will learn about some security related tips in the following "Don't use Output Cache".

81. What is Bundling and Minification in MVC?

Bundling and minification are two new techniques introduced to improve request load time. It improves load time by reducing the number of requests to the server and reducing the size of requested assets (such as CSS and JavaScript).

Bundling

It lets us combine multiple JavaScript (.js) files or multiple cascading style sheet (.css) files so that they can be downloaded as a unit, rather than making individual HTTP requests.

Minification

It squeezes out whitespace and performs other types of compression to make the downloaded files as small as possible. At runtime, the process identifies the user agent, for example IE, Mozilla, etc. and then removes whatever is specific to Mozilla when the request comes from IE.

82. What is Validation Summary in MVC?

The ValidationSummary helper method generates an unordered list (ul element) of validation messages that are in the ModelStateDictionary object.

The ValidationSummary can be used to display all the error messages for all the fields. It can also be used to display custom error messages. The following figure shows how ValidationSummary displays the error messages.

Edit

Student

- The Name field is required.
- The Age field is required.

Name [   ]

Age [   ]

[Save]

ValidationSummary() Signature

MvcHtmlStringValidateMessage(bool excludePropertyErrors, string message, object htmlAttributes)

Display field level error messages using ValidationSummary

By default, ValidationSummary filters out field level error messages. If you want to display field level error messages as a summary then specify *excludePropertyErrors = false.*

Example - ValidationSummary to display field errors

@Html.ValidationSummary(false, "", new { @class = "text-danger" })

So now, the following Edit view will display error messages as a summary at the top. Please make sure that you don't have a ValidationMessageFor method for each of the fields.

83. What is Database First Approach in MVC using Entity Framework?

Database First Approach is an alternative to the Code First and Model First approaches to the Entity Data Model which creates model codes (classes,properties, DbContextetc) from the database in the project and that classes behaves as the link between database and controller.

There are the following approach which is used to connect with database to application.

- Database First
- Model First
- Code First

Database first is nothing but only a approach to create web application where database is available first and can interact with the database. In this database, database is created first and after that we manage the code. The Entity Framework is able to generate a business model based on the tables and columns in a relational database.

84. What are the Folders in MVC application solutions?

Understanding the folders

When you create a project a folder structure gets created by default under the name of your project which can be seen in solution explorer. Below i will give you a brief explanation of what these folders are for.

Model

This folder contains classes that is used to provide data. These classes can contain data that is retrived from the database or data inserted in the form by the user to update the database.

Controllers

These are the classes which will perform the action invoked by the user. These classes contains methods known as "Actions" which responds to the user action accordingly.

Views

These are simple pages which uses the model class data to populate the HTML controls and renders it to the client browser.

App_Start

Contains Classes such as FilterConfig, RoutesConfig, WebApiConfig. As of now we need to understand the RouteConfig class. This class contains the default format of the url that should be supplied in the browser to navigate to a specified page.

85. What are the methods of handling an Error in MVC?

Exception handling may be required in any application, whether it is a web application or a Windows Forms application.

ASP.Net MVC has an attribute called "HandleError" that provides built-in exception filters. The HandleError attribute in ASP.NET MVC can be applied over the action method as well as Controller or at the global level. The HandleError attribute is the default implementation of IExceptionFilter. When we create a MVC application, the HandleError attribute is added within the Global.asax.cs file and registered in the Application_Start event.

```
1.  public static void RegisterGlobalFilters(GlobalFilterCollection filters)
2.  {
3.      filters.Add(new HandleErrorAttribute());
4.  }
5.  protected void Application_Start()
6.  {
7.      AreaRegistration.RegisterAllAreas();
8.      RegisterGlobalFilters(GlobalFilters.Filters);
9.      RegisterRoutes(RouteTable.Routes);
10. }
```

Important properties of HandleError attribute

The HandleError Error attribute has a couple for properties that are very useful in handling the exception.

ExceptionType

Type of exception to be catch. If this property is not specified then the HandleError filter handles all exceptions.

View

Name of the view page for displaying the exception information.

Master

Master View for displaying the exception.

Order

Order in which the action filters are executed. The Order property has an integer value and it specifies the priority from 1 to any positive integer value. 1 means highest priority and the greater the value of the integer is, the lower is the priority of the filter.

AllowMultiple

It indicates whether more than one instance of the error filter attribute can be specified.

Example

```
1.  [HandleError(View = "Error")]
2.  public class HomeController: Controller
3.  {
4.     public ActionResult Index()
5.     {
6.        ViewBag.Message = "Welcome to ASP.NET MVC!";
7.        int u = Convert.ToInt32(""); // Error line
8.        return View();
9.     }
10.}
```

HandleError Attribute at Action Method Level,

```
1.  [HandleError(View = "Error")]
2.  public ActionResult Index()
3.  {
4.     ViewBag.Message = "Welcome to ASP.NET MVC!";
5.     int u = Convert.ToInt32(""); // Error line
6.     return View();
7.  }
```

86.How can we pass the data From Controller To View In MVC?

There are three options in Model View Controller (MVC) for passing data from controller to view. This article attempts to explain the differences among ViewData, ViewBag and TempData with examples. ViewData and ViewBag are similar and TempData performs additional responsibility. The following are the key points on those three objects.

ViewData

- The ViewData is used to move data from controller to view.

- The ViewData is a dictionary of objects that are derived from the "ViewDataDictionary" class and it will be accessible using strings as keys.
- ViewData contains a null value when redirection occurs.
- ViewData requires typecasting for complex data types.

ViewBag

- ViewBag is just a dynamic wrapper around ViewData and exists only in ASP.NET MVC 3. ViewBag is a dynamic property that takes advantage of the new dynamic features in C# 4.0.
- ViewBag doesn't require typecasting for complex data types.
- ViewBag also contain a null value when redirection occurs.

TempData

- ViewData moves data from controller to view.
- Use TempData when you need data to be available for the next request, only. In the next request, it will be there but will be gone after that.
- TempData is used to pass data from the current request to the subsequent request, in other words in case of redirection. That means the value of TempData will not be null.

87.What is JsonResultType in MVC?

Action methods on controllers return JsonResult (JavaScript Object Notation result) that can be used in an AJAX application. This class is inherited from the "ActionResult" abstract class. Here Json is provided one argument which must be serializable. The JSON result object that serializes the specified object to JSON format.

```
1. public JsonResult JsonResultTest()
2. {
3.     return Json("Hello My Friend!");
4. }
```

88. What is Data Annotation Validator Attributes in MVC?

Using the Data Annotation Validator Attributes

DataAnnotation plays a vital role in added validation to properties while designing the model itself. This validation can be added for both the client side and the server side.

You understand that decorating the properties in a model with an Attribute can make that property eligible for Validation.

Some of the DataAnnotation used for validation are given below,

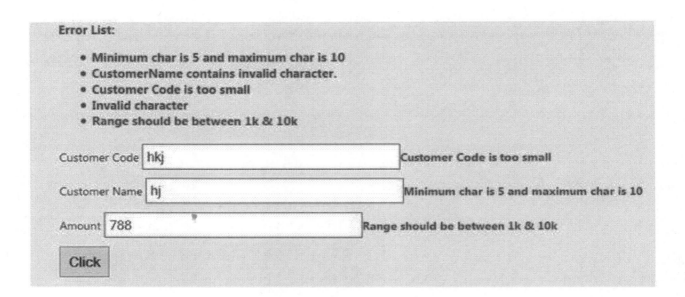

1. *Required*
   Specify a property as required.
   1. [Required(ErrorMessage="CustomerName is mandatory")]

2. *RegularExpression*
   Specifies the regular expression to validate the value of the property.
   1. [RegularExpression("[a-z]", ErrorMessage = "Invalid character")]

3. *Range*

Specifies the Range of values between which the property values are checked.

1. [Range(1000,10000,ErrorMessage="Range should be between 1k & 10k")]

4. *StringLength*

Specifies the Min & Max length for a string property.

1. [StringLength(50, MinimumLength = 5, ErrorMessage = "Minimum char is 5 and maximum char is 10")]

5. *MaxLength*

Specifies the Max length for the property value.

1. [MaxLength(10,ErrorMessage="Customer Code is exceeding")]

6. *MinLength*

It is used to check for minimum length.

1. [MinLength(5, ErrorMessage = "Customer Code is too small")]

89.How can we show Custom Error Page in MVC?

The HandleErrorAttribute allows you to use a custom page for this error. First you need to update your web.config file to allow your application to handle custom errors.

```
1. <system.web>
2.    <customErrors mode="On">
3. </system.web>
```

Then, your action method needs to be marked with the atttribute.

```
1. [HandleError]
2. public class HomeController: Controller
3. {
4.    [HandleError]
5.    publicActionResultThrowException()
6.    {
7.       throw new ApplicationException();
8.    }
```

9. }

By calling the ThrowException action, this would then redirect the user to the default error page. In our case though, we want to use a custom error page and redirect the user there instead.So, let's create our new custom view page.

```
<%@ Page Language="C#" Inherits="System.Web.Mvc.ViewPage" %>

<!DOCTYPE html PUBLIC "-//W3C//DTD XHTML 1.0 Transitional//EN" "http://t
<html xmlns="http://www.w3.org/1999/xhtml">
<head runat="server">
    <title>CustomErrorView</title>
</head>
<body>
    <h2>
        Error</h2>
    <p>
        Controller:
        <%=((HandleErrorInfo)ViewData.Model).ControllerName %>
    </p>
    <p>
        Action:
        <%=((HandleErrorInfo)ViewData.Model).ActionName %>
    </p>
    <p>
        Message:
        <%=((HandleErrorInfo)ViewData.Model).Exception.Message %>
    </p>
    <p>
        Stack Trace:
        <%=((HandleErrorInfo)ViewData.Model).Exception.StackTrace %>
    </p>
</body>
</html>
```

Next, we simply need to update the HandleErrorAttribute on the action method.

```
1. [HandleError]
2. public class HomeController: Controller
3. {
4.     [HandleError(View = "CustomErrorView")]
5.     publicActionResultThrowException()
6.     {
```

```
7.        throw new ApplicationException();
8.     }
9.  }
```

90.Server Side Validation in MVC?

The ASP.NET MVC Framework validates any data passed to the controller action that is executing, It populates a ModelState object with any validation failures that it finds and passes that object to the controller. Then the controller actions can query the ModelState to discover whether the request is valid and react accordingly.

I will use two approaches in this article to validate a model data. One is to manually add an error to the ModelState object and another uses the Data Annotation API to validate the model data.

Approach 1 - Manually Add Error to ModelState object

I create a User class under the Models folder. The User class has two properties "Name" and "Email". The "Name" field has required field validations while the "Email" field has Email validation. So let's see the procedure to implement the validation. Create the User Model as in the following,

```
1.  namespace ServerValidation.Models
2.  {
3.      public class User
4.      {
5.          public string Name
6.          {
7.              get;
8.              set;
9.          }
10.         public string Email
11.         {
```

```
12.        get;
13.        set;
14.    }
15.  }
16.}
```

After that I create a controller action in User Controller (UserController.cs under Controllers folder). That action method has logic for the required validation for Name and Email validation on the Email field. I add an error message on ModelState with a key and that message will be shown on the view whenever the data is not to be validated in the model.

```
1.  using System.Text.RegularExpressions;
2.  using System.Web.Mvc;
3.  namespace ServerValidation.Controllers
4.  {
5.      public class UserController: Controller
6.      {
7.          public ActionResult Index()
8.          {
9.              return View();
10.         }
11.         [HttpPost]
12.      public ActionResult Index(ServerValidation.Models.User model)
13.         {
14.
15.          if (string.IsNullOrEmpty(model.Name))
16.          {
17.              ModelState.AddModelError("Name", "Name is required");
18.          }
19.          if (!string.IsNullOrEmpty(model.Email))
20.          {
21.              string emailRegex = @ "^([a-zA-Z0-9_\-\.]+)@((\[[0-9]{1,3}" +
22.              @ "\.[0-9]{1,3}\.[0-9]{1,3}\.)|(([a-zA-Z0-9\-]+\" +
23.              @ ".)+))([a-zA-Z]{2,4}|[0-9]{1,3})(\]?)$";
24.          Regex re = new Regex(emailRegex);
25.          if (!re.IsMatch(model.Email))
26.          {
27.              ModelState.AddModelError("Email", "Email is not valid");
```

```
28.            }
29.         } else {
30.             ModelState.AddModelError("Email", "Email is required");
31.         }
32.         if (ModelState.IsValid)
33.         {
34.             ViewBag.Name = model.Name;
35.             ViewBag.Email = model.Email;
36.         }
37.         return View(model);
38.     }
39.  }
40.}
```

Thereafter I create a view (Index.cshtml) for the user input under the User folder.

```
1.  @model ServerValidation.Models.User
2.  @ {
3.      ViewBag.Title = "Index";
4.  }
5.  @using(Html.BeginForm())
6.  {
7.      if (@ViewData.ModelState.IsValid)
8.      {
9.          if (@ViewBag.Name != null)
10.     { < b >
11.             Name: @ViewBag.Name < br / >
12.             Email: @ViewBag.Email < /b>
13.         }
14.     } < fieldset >
15.         < legend > User < /legend>  < div class = "editor-label" >
16.         @Html.LabelFor(model => model.Name) < /div> < div class = "ed
itor-field" >
17.         @Html.EditorFor(model => model.Name)
18.     @if(!ViewData.ModelState.IsValid)
19. {
20. < span class = "field-validation-
error" > @ViewData.ModelState["Name"].Errors[0].ErrorMessage < /
span>
21.
```

227

```
22.}
23.< /div>  < div class = "editor-label" >
24.

25.       @Html.LabelFor(model => model.Email) < /div> < div class = "ed
   itor-field" >
26.       @Html.EditorFor(model => model.Email)
27.   @if(!ViewData.ModelState.IsValid)
28. {
29.< span class = "field-validation-
   error" > @ViewData.ModelState["Email"].Errors[0].ErrorMessage < /
   span>
30.  }
31. < /div> < p >
32.    < input type = "submit"
33.   value = "Create" / >
34.     < /p> < /fieldset>
35.}
```

91. What is the use of remote validation in MVC?

Remote validation is the process where we validate specific data posting data to a server without posting the entire form data to the server. Let's see an actual scenario, in one of my projects I had a requirement to validate an email address, whetehr it already exists in the database. Remote validation was useful for that; without posting all the data we can validate only the email address supplied by the user.

Practical Explanation

Let's create a MVC project and name it accordingly, for me its "TestingRemoteValidation". Once the project is created let's create a model named UserModel that will look like:

```
1.  public class UserModel
2.  {
3.     [Required]
```

```
4.    public string UserName
5.    {
6.       get;
7.       set;
8.    }
9.    [Remote("CheckExistingEmail", "Home", ErrorMessage = "Email alre
      ady exists!")]
10.   public string UserEmailAddress
11.   {
12.      get;
13.      set;
14.   }
15. }
```

Let's get some understanding of the remote attribute used, so the very first parameter "CheckExistingEmail" is the the name of the action. The second parameter "Home" is referred to as controller so to validate the input for the UserEmailAddress the "CheckExistingEmail" action of the "Home" controller is called and the third parameter is the error message. Let's implement the "CheckExistingEmail" action result in our home controller.

```
1.  public ActionResult CheckExistingEmail(string UserEmailAddress)
2.  {
3.     bool ifEmailExist = false;
4.     try
5.     {
6.        ifEmailExist = UserEmailAddress.Equals("mukeshknayak@gmail.c
      om") ? true : false;
7.        return Json(!ifEmailExist, JsonRequestBehavior.AllowGet);
8.     } catch (Exception ex)
9.     {
10.       return Json(false, JsonRequestBehavior.AllowGet);
11.    }
12. }
```

92.What are the Exception filters in MVC?

Exception are part and parcel of an application. They are a boon and a ban for an application too. Isn't it? This would be controversial, for developers it helps them track minor and major defects in an application and sometimes they are frustrating when it lets users land on the Yellow screen of death each time. This would make the users mundane to the application. Thus to avoid this, developers handle the exceptions. But still sometimes there are a few unhandled exceptions.

Now what is to be done for them? MVC provides us with built-in "Exception Filters" about which we will explain here.

Let's start!

A Yellow screen of Death can be said is as a wardrobe malfunction of our application.

Get Started

Exception filters run when some of the exceptions are unhandled and thrown from an invoked action. The reason for the exception can be anything and so is the source of the exception.

Creating an Exception Filter

Custom Exception Filters must implement the builtinIExceptionFilter interface. The interface looks as in the following,

```
1.  public interface IExceptionFilter
2.  {
3.      void OnException(ExceptionContext filterContext)
4.  }
```

Whenever an unhandled exception is encountered, the OnException method gets invoked. The parameter as we can see, ExceptionContext is derived from the ControllerContext and has a number of built-in properties that can be used to get the information about the request causing the exception. Their property's ExceptionContextpassess are shown in the following table:

Result   :ActionResult:The result returned by the action being invoked.

Exception:Exception:The unhandled exceptions caused from the actions in the applications.

ExceptionHandled: BOOL   :This is a very handy property that returns a bool value (true/false) based on if the exception is handled by any of the filters in the applicaiton or not.

The exception being thrown from the action is detailed by the Exception property and once handled (if), then the property ExceptionHandled can be toggled, so that the other filters would know if the exception has been already handled and cancel the other filter requests to handle. The problem is that if the exceptions are not handled, then the default MVC behavior shows the dreaded yellow screen of death. To the users, that makes a very impression on the users and more importantly, it exposes the application's handy and secure information to the outside world that may have hackers and then the application gets into the road to hell. Thus, the exceptions need to be dealt with very carefully. Let's show one small custom exception filter. This filter can be stored inside the Filters folder in the web project of the solution. Let's add a file/class called CustomExceptionFilter.cs.

```
1.  public class CustomExceptionFilter: FilterAttribute,
2.      IExceptionFilter
3.  {
4.          public void OnException(ExceptionContext filterContext)
5.          {
6.          if (!filterContext.ExceptionHandled && filterContext.Exception is
    NullReferenceException)
7.              {
```

```
8.          filterContext.Result = new RedirectResult("customErrorPage.
   html");
9.          filterContext.ExceptionHandled = true;
10.        }
11.    }
12. }
```

93.Explain RenderSection in MVC?

RenderSection() is a method of the WebPageBase class. Scott wrote at one point, The first parameter to the "RenderSection()" helper method specifies the name of the section we want to render at that location in the layout template. The second parameter is optional, and allows us to define whether the section we are rendering is required or not. If a section is "required", then Razor will throw an error at runtime if that section is not implemented within a view template that is based on the layout file (that can make it easier to track down content errors). It returns the HTML content to render.

```
1. <div id="body">
2.    @RenderSection("featured", required: false)
3.    <section class="content-wrapper main-content clear-fix">
4.       @RenderBody()
5.    </section>
6. </div>
```

94.What is GET and POST Actions Types?

GET

GET is used to request data from a specified resource. With all the GET request we pass the URL which is compulsory, however it can take the following overloads.

.get(url [, data] [, success(data, textStatus, jqXHR)] [, dataType]).done/.fail

POST

POST is used to submit data to be processed to a specified resource. With all the POST requests we pass the URL which is compulsory and the data, however it can take the following overloads.

.post(url [, data] [, success(data, textStatus, jqXHR)] [, dataType])

95.What's new in MVC 6?

In MVC 6 Microsoft removed the dependency of System.Web.Dll from MVC6 because it's so expensive that typically it consume 30k of memory per request and response, whereas now MVC 6 only requires 2k of memory per request and the response is a very small memory consumtion.

The advantage of using the cloud-optimized framework is that we can include a copy of the mono CLR with your website. For the sake of one website we do not need to upgrade the .NET version on the entire machine. A different version of the CLR for a different website running side by side.

MVC 6 is a part of ASP.NET 5 that has been designed for cloud-optimized applications. The runtime automatically picks the correct version of the library when our MVC application is deployed to the cloud.

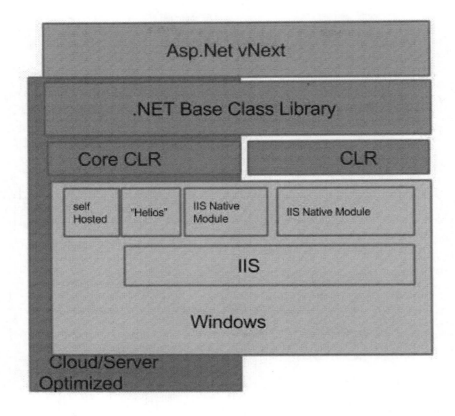

The Core CLR is also supposed to be tuned with a high resource-efficient optimization.

Microsoft has made many MVC, Web API, WebPage and SignalLrpeices we call MVC 6.

Most of the problems are solved using the Roslyn Compiler. In ASP.NET vNext uses the Roslyn Compiler. Using the Roslyn Compiler we do not need to compile the application, it automatically compiles the application code. You will edit a code file and can then see the changes by refreshing the browser without stopping or rebuilding the project.

Run on hosts other than IIS

Where we use MVC5 we can host it on an IIS server and we can also run it on top of an ASP. NET Pipeline, on the other hand MVC 6 has a feature that makes it better and that feature is itself hosted on an IIS server and a self-user pipeline.

Environment based configuration system

The configuration system provides an environment to easily deploy the application on the cloud. Our application works just like a configuration provider. It helps to retrieve the value from the various configuration sources like XML file.

MVC 6 includes a new environment-based configuration system. Unlike something else it depends on just the Web.Config file in the previous version.

Dependency injection

Using the IServiceProvider interface we can easily add our own dependency injection container. We can replace the default implementation with our own container.

Supports OWIN

We have complete control over the composable pipeline in MVC 6 applications. MVC 6 supports the OWIN abstraction.

WEB API

1. What is ASP.Net Web API?
Web API is the Microsoft open source technology to develop REST services which is based on HTTP protocol. ASP.Net Web API is a framework to build, consume HTTP based service. Web API can be consumed by a wide range of clients such as web browser and mobile applications.

2. Web API vs WCF REST API.
WCF REST API is good for Message Queue, duplex communication, one way

messaging. Web API is good for HTTP based service.
Web API is the best fit with MVC pattern which is the major benefits of the Web API.
WCF will support SOAP and XML format, while Web API can support any media format including JSON, XML.
WCF is good for developing service oriented applications and ASP.Net Web API is perfect for building HTTP services.
WCF can support HTTP, TCP, Named Pipes as protocol on another side Web API can support HTTP protocol only.
WEB API is easy for experienced developers in MVC pattern.
WCF requires lots of configuration to run, while Web API is simple and no configuration required to run.

WCF
1. It is a framework used to build or develop service-oriented applications.
2. WCF will only be consumed by clients, which will understand XML. WCF can support protocols such as – HTTP, TCP, Named Pipes etc.

Web API
1. It is a framework that will help us for building/developing HTTP services
2. Web API is an open source platform.
3. It will support most of the MVC features that will keep Web API over WCF.

3. The advantage of Web API over WCF services.
The disadvantage of WCF over Web API is that WCF will require a lot of configuration to work, but in Web API is simple and no extra configuration.

4. Advantages of using ASP.Net Web API.
Using ASP.NET Web API has following advantages :
1. It will work as HTTP works using standard HTTP verbs like GET, POST, PUT, DELETE, etc. for all CRUD operations
2. Complete support for routing
3. Response will be generated in JSON or XML format using MediaTypeFormatter
4. It has the ability to be hosted in IIS and self-host outside of IIS
5. Supports Model binding and Validation
6. Support for OData

5. What are the various return types in ASP.Net Web API?
Following are the various return types in ASP.Net Web API
1. HttpResponseMessage
2. IHttpActionResult
3. Void

4. Other Type – string, int, or other entity types.

6. What is ASP.Net Web API routing?
Routing in ASP.Net Web API is the process that will decide which action and which controller should be called.
There are following ways to implement routing in Web API.
1. Convention based routing
2. Attribute based routing

7. What are Media type formatter in Web API?
Following are Media type formatter in Web API:
1. MediaTypeFormatter – Base class for handling serializing and deserializing strongly-typed objects.
2. BefferedMediaTypeFormatter – Represents a helper class for allowing asynchronous formatter on top of the asynchronous formatter infrastructure.

8. CORS issue in Web API?
CORS will stand for Cross-Origin Resource Sharing. CORS will resolve the same-origin restriction for JavaScript. The same Origin means that a JavaScript will only make AJAX call for the web pages within the same origin.
We must install CORS nuget package using Package Manager Console to enable CORS in Web API.
Open WebAPIConfig.cs file
add config.EnableCors();

Add EnableCors attribute to the Controller class and define the origin.

[EnableCors(origins: "", headers: "*", methods: "*")].

9. How to secure an ASP.Net Web API?
Web API security means, We required to control Web API and decide who can access the API and who will not access the Web API.
using Token based authentication .Setting proper authentication and authorization makes it safe.

10. Http Get vs Http Post
GET and POST is two important HTTP verbs. HTTP (HyperText Transfer Protocol) can manage the request-response between client and server.
GET parameters is included in URL
POST parameter is included in the body

Get request will not make any changes to the server
POST is for making changes to the server

GET request is idempotent
POST request is non-idempotent.
In a GET request, we will send data in plain text.
In a POST request, we will send binary as well as text data.

11. Can Web API be used with traditional ASP.Net Forms?
Yes, Web API will be used with ASP.Net Forms.
We will add Web API Controller and manage to route in Application Start method in Global.asax file.

12. Exception filters in ASP.Net Web API
Exception filter in Web API will implement IExceptionFilters interface. Web API Exception filters can execute when an action will throw an exception at any stage.

13. Do we return View from ASP.Net Web API?
No, it will not be possible in Web API as Web API will create HTTP based service. It is available in MVC application.

14. What's new in ASP.Net Web API 2.0?
The following features are introduced in ASP.NET Web API framework v2.0:
1. Attribute Routing
2. External Authentication
3. CORS (Cross-Origin Resource Sharing)
4. OWIN (Open Web Interface for .NET) Self Hosting
5. IHttpActionResult
6. Web API OData
Following new features are included in Web API 2 –
1. Attribute-based routing
Route("product/{productid}/category")]
public string Get(int productid)
{
return "value";
}
2. CORS (Cross-Origin Resource Sharing) support
3. OWIN to Self Host Web API
4. Web API OData

15. How do we restrict access to methods with an HTTP verb in Web API?

We will just add an attribute as shown below –

```
[HttpGet]
public HttpResponseMessage Test()
{
HttpResponseMessage response = new HttpResponseMessage();
///
return response;
}
[HttpPost]
public void Save([FromBody]string value)
{

}
```

16. How do we make sure that Web API returns data in JSON format only?

To make sure that web API returns data in JSON format only this open "WebApiConfig.cs" file and add below line :

```
config.Formatters.JsonFormatter.SupportedMediaTypes.Add(new
MediaTypeHeaderValue("application/json"))
```

17.How to provide Alias name for an action method in Web API?

We can provide Alias name by adding an attribute ActionName
[ActionName("InertUserData")]

```
// POST api/
public void Post([FromBody]string value)
{
}
```

18. How we can handle errors in Web API?

Following classes will help to handle the exception in ASP.Net Web API.
1. ExceptionFilters
2. HttpError
3. HttpResponseException

19. How to host Web API?

Web API application will be hosted in two ways :

1. Self Hosting – Web API will be hosted in Console Application or Windows Service.
2. IIS Hosting – Web API will also be hosted with IIS and the process can be similar to hosting a website.

20. How to consume Web API using HttpClient?

HttpClient will be introduced in HttpClient class for communicating with ASP.Net Web API. This HttpClient class will be used in a console application or in an MVC application.

Using Entity Framework, the implementation of Web API CRUD operation in MVC application .

21. Parameters in Web API

Action methods in Web API will accept parameters as a query string in URL or it will accept with the request body.

For example to fetch particular product details the Get method will require an id parameter.

```
public IHttpActionResult GetProductMaster(int id)
{
ProductMaster productMaster = db.ProductMasters.Find(id);
if (productMaster == null)
{
return NotFound();
}
return Ok(productMaster);
}
```

In the same way, the Post method will require complex type parameter to post data to the server.

```
public IHttpActionResult PostProductMaster(ProductMaster productMaster)
{
if (!ModelState.IsValid)
{
return BadRequest(ModelState);
}

db.ProductMasters.Add(productMaster);
db.SaveChanges();
```

```
return CreatedAtRoute("DefaultApi", new { id = productMaster.id },
productMaster);
}
```
Similarly PUT method will require primitive data type example for id and
complex parameter i.e. ProductMaster class.
```
if (id != productMaster.id)
{
return BadRequest();
}

db.Entry(productMaster).State = EntityState.Modified;

try
{
db.SaveChanges();
}
catch (DbUpdateConcurrencyException)
{
if (!ProductMasterExists(id))
{
return NotFound();
}
else
{
throw;
}
}
return StatusCode(HttpStatusCode.NoContent);
}
```

22. Explain oData with ASP.Net Web API.
OData is stand for Open Data Protocol, it will be a Rest-based data access
protocol. OData will provide a way for querying and manipulating data using
CRUD operation. ASP.Net Web API will support OData V3 and V4.
For using OData in ASP.Net Web API, We required the OData package by
running below command in Package Manager Console.

Install-Package Microsoft.AspNet.Odata

23. Can we consume Web API 2 in C# console application?

Yes, we consume Web API 2 in Console Application, Angular JS, MVC or any other application.

24. Perform Web API 2 CRUD operation using Entity Framework.

We can perform CRUD operation using entity framework with Web API. We will read one of my blog for seeing the implementation of Web API 2 CRUD operation using Entity Framework.

25. How to Enable HTTPS in Web API?

Steps to enable HTTPS in ASP.NET Web API,

- Write a custom class which is inherited from AuthorizationFilterAttribute
- Register that class in ASP.NET Web API Config
- Apply [RequireHttps] attribute on API controller actions.
- Create a temporary certificate for SSL.
- Install the certificate
- Enable HTTPS support to the development server in Visual Studio.

Write a custom class which is inherited from AuthorizationFilterAttribute

Write a custom class as shown below.

```
1.  public class RequireHttpsAttribute: AuthorizationFilterAttribute
2.  {
3.      public override void OnAuthorization (HttpActionContext actionContext)
4.      {
5.          if (actionContext.Request.RequestUri.Scheme ! = Uri.UriSchemeHttps)
6.          {
7.              actionContext.Response = new HttpResponseMessage (System.Net.HttpStatusCode.Forbidden)
8.              {
9.                  ReasonPhrase = "HTTPS Required for this call"
10.             };
11.         }
12.         else
13.         {
14.             base.OnAuthorization(actionContext);
```

```
15.       }
16.    }
17. }
```

Register that class in ASP.NET Web API Config

To register custom HTTP filter class in web API configuration here are the settings.

```
1.  // Web API configuration and services
2.    config.Filters.Add(new RequireHttpsAttribute());
```

Remember this a global setting and will require all controller methods to run on HTTPS.

If we want to have a few methods to run on HTTP then in that case, just disable this setting. And use the [Requirehttps] attribute for individual methods.

Apply [RequireHttps] attribute on API controller actions.

```
1.  [RequireHttps]
2.  public IEnumerable<string> Get ()
3.  {
4.      return new string [] { "value1", "value2" };
5.  }
```

Note
We need to use this [RequireHttps] attribute only in case we need to enable HTTPS only for selective API controller actions. Otherwise Web API configuration global settings are enough.

But if are targeting only a few API methods to run on HTTPS then we must disable the global configuration. Otherwise, all method calls will demand HTTPS.

Create a temporary certificate for SSL

To create a temp certificate run the following command in the command prompt.

makecert.exe -n "CN=Development CA" -r -sv TempCA.pvk TempCA.cer

Once the certificate is created it will be saved on your machine at the path selected in the command prompt windows.

Now, we need to install it.

Install the certificate

For installing the certificate on your local machine, you need to do the following steps.

- Open MMC (Management console) window
- Then go to File - > Add or Remove Snap Ins
- Then select Certificates from available Snap Ins
- Then click on the ADD button
- Then select Computer account in the window pane that opens
- Then select Local Computer Account
- Then click next and OK

Now the certificate snap is added to MMC.

Now we need to install the certificate by selecting it in a snap.

For that,

- Go to Certificates; expand it.
- Then Select "Trusted root certification Authorities"
- Then Select Action - > All Tasks - > Imports
- Select the certificate and finish.

Now, a temporary certificate is installed on your computer.

This certificate will be used for SSL communication on your machine, but apart from installation, you don't need to do anything with respect to certificates.

Now, the next step is to enable Https for the development server.

Enable HTTPS support to development server in Visual Studio

For that do the following:

- Open your web API solution in Visual Studio,

- Then select the web API project in Solution Explorer.
- Select View Menu in Visual Studio
- Now select "Properties window" or click F4.
- A window pane will open.
- There select "SSL Enabled" property and set it to true

Now, the development server is ready to work with HTTPS too.

26. How to implement Basic Authentication in ASP.Net Web API?
Basic Authentication is a simple authentication mechanism where the client will send request with an Authorization header with word Basic. In Basic Authentication, Authorization header will contain a word Basic followed by base 64 encoded string.
The syntax for Basic Authentication –

Authorization: Basic username: password

27. What is Token Based Authentication in Web API?
A better approach for securing .Net Web API is by authenticating users by a signed token which is called token-based approach.
In Token-based authentication –
A client will send a request to the server with the credential. If the provided credential is valid then the server will send a token to the client.
This token will contain user details for the identification with an expiry time. Once the client will received the token, it will use this token to access API resources wherever authentication requires.
To implement Token-based authentication we need to install Microsoft.Owin from Nuget package.

28. What is content negotiation in .Net Web API?
In ASP.Net Web API, content negotiation will be performed at the server-side. This is for determining the media type formatter for returning the response to an incoming request.

29. What is ASP.Net identity?
ASP.Net identity is the membership management framework provided by Microsoft which will be easily integrated with Web API. This will help us in building a secure HTTP service.

30. What is Bearer Authenticating in .Net Web API?
Bearer authentication is also called as Token-based authentication.

31. What is Rest?

REST is stand for Representational State Transfer. This is an architectural pattern to exchange data over a distributed environment. REST architectural pattern can treat each service as a resource and a client will access these resources by using HTTP protocol methods such as GET, POST, PUT, and DELETE.

32.What is Not Rest?

Following is Not Rest:

1. A protocol
2. A standard
3.A replacement of SOAP

33. When to choose WCF and Web API over the other?

WCF (Windows Communication Foundation) is available in .NET to create both SOAP and REST services. A lot of configuration is needed to turn a WCF service into a REST service. To create REST services is ASP.NET Web API is better choice.

WCF is suited to build services which are **transport/protocol** independent. For example, we want to build a single service which can be consumed by 2 different clients – a Java client and .NET client. Java client will want the transport protocol to be HTTP and message format to be XML for interoperability, whereas the .NET client will expect the protocol to be TCP and the message format to be binary for performance. WCF is the right choice for this. Create a single WCF service, and configure 2 endpoints one for each client (one for the Java client and the other for the .NET client).

It is a bit more complex and configuration can be a headache to use WCF to create REST services. If we are stuck with .NET 3.5 or we have an existing SOAP service we should support but required to add REST to reach more clients, then use WCF.

If we will not have the limitation of .NET 3.5 and we required to create a brand new restful service then use ASP.NET Web API.

34. When do we need to choose Web API?

Today, a web-based application is not sufficient to reach its customers. Peoples are using iPhone, mobile, tablets etc. devices in their daily life. These devices will have a lot of apps to make their life easy. Actually, we are moving towards apps world.

Therefore, if we want for exposing our service data to the browsers to all these modern devices apps in a fast and simple way, we will have an API which will be compatible with browsers as well as all these devices.

The ASP.NET WEB API is a great framework to build HTTP services which will be consumed by a broad range of clients including browsers, mobiles, iPhone and tablets. WEB API is open source and an ideal platform to build REST-full services over the .NET Framework.

35. What are RESTful services?

REST is stand for Representational State Transfer. The REST was first introduced in the year 2000 by Roy Fielding as part of his doctoral dissertation. REST is an architectural pattern to exchange the data over a distributed environment. REST architectural pattern will treat each service as a resource and a client will access these resources by using HTTP protocol methods such as GET, POST, PUT, and DELETE. The REST architectural pattern will specific a set of constraints which a system should adhere to. Following are the REST constraints:

1. Client-Server constraint –

This is the first constraint. This constraint will specify which a Client will send a request to the server and the server will send a response back to the client. This separation of concerns can support the independent development of both client-side and server-side logic. That means client application and server application can be developed separately without any dependency on each other. A client will only know resource URIs and that's all. Severs and clients will also be replaced and developed independently as long as the interface between them will not be altered.

Stateless constraint –

The next constraint is the stateless constraint. The stateless constraint will specify that the communication between the client and the server should be stateless between requests. We will not be storing anything on the server related to the client. The request from the client will contain all the necessary information for the server for processing that request. This will ensure that each request will be treated independently by the server.

Cacheable constraint –

Some data will be provided by the server such as the list of products, or list of departments in a company will not change that often. This constraint states that let the client know how long this data will be good for therefore the client will not have to come back to the server for that data over and over again.

Uniform Interface constraint –

The uniform interface constraint will define an interface between the client and the server. To understand the uniform interface constraint, we required to understand what a resource is and the HTTP verbs – GET, PUT, POST and DELETE. In the context of a REST API, resources typically represent data entities. The product, Employee, Customer, etc. are all resources. The HTTP verb (GET, PUT, POST, and DELETE) which is sent with each request informs the API what to do with the resource. Each resource will be identified by a specific URI (Uniform Resource Identifier).

Layered System-
REST will allow us to use a layered system architecture where we can deploy the APIs in server A, and will store data on server B and authenticate requests in server C. For example, a client will not ordinarily state whether it will be connected directly to the server or to an intermediary along the way.
1. SOAP Performance is slow as compared to REST.

36. What are the differences between REST and SOAP?
The difference between REST and SOAP is following:
1. SOAP will stand for Simple Object Access Protocol whereas REST stands for Representational State Transfer.
2. The SOAP is an XML which is based protocol whereas REST will not a protocol but it is an architectural pattern example for resource-based architecture.
3. SOAP has specifications for both stateless and state-full implementation whereas REST will be completely stateless.
4. SOAP will enforce message format as XML whereas REST will not enforce message format as XML or JSON.
5. The SOAP message is consist of an envelope that will include SOAP headers and body for storing the actual information we required for sending whereas REST will use the HTTP build-in headers with a variety of media-types for storing the information and it will use the HTTP GET, POST, PUT and DELETE methods for performing CRUD operations.
6. SOAP will use interfaces and named operations for exposing the service whereas to expose resources (service) REST will use URI and methods such as GET, PUT, POST, DELETE.

37. What are the differences between ASP.NET MVC and ASP.NET Web API?

Following are some of the differences between MVC and Web API
MVC
1. MVC is used for creating a web app, in which we will build web pages.
2. For JSON it can return JSONResult from an action method.
3. All requests will be mapped to the respective action methods.
Web API
1. This is used for creating a service using HTTP verbs

2. This will return XML or JSON to the client.

3. All request will be mapped to actions using HTTP verbs.

There are some following differences between ASP.NET MVC and WEB API:

1. MVC can be used for creating web applications which will return both views and data but ASP.NET WEB API will be used for creating rest full HTTP services with the easy and simple way which will return only data, not view.

2. WEB API will help for building REST-full services over the .NET Framework and it will also support content-negotiation that is not in MVC.

3. WEB API will also take care of returning data in a particular format such as JSON, XML or any other based upon the Accept header in the request. MVC return data in JSON format using JsonResult.

4. In WEB API the request will be mapped to the actions based on HTTP verbs but in MVC it will be mapped to actions name.

5. We will mix WEB API and MVC controller in a single project for handling advanced AJAX requests which will return data in JSON, XML or any others format and building a full-blown HTTP service. Typically, this can be called WEB API self-hosting.

6. WEB API is lightweight architecture and will except the web application, it will also be used with smartphone apps.

38. Is it true that ASP.NET Web API has replaced WCF?

No, t ASP.NET Web API has not replaced WCF. It is an other way of building non-SOAP based services, for example, plain XML or JSON string, etc.

Yes, it will have some added advantages such as utilizing the full features of HTTP and reaching more clients like mobile devices, etc.

WCF is a better choice for the following scenarios:

1. If we are intended to use transport other than HTTP, example for TCP, UDP or Named Pipes

2. Message Queuing scenario will be using MSMQ.

3. One-way communication or Duplex communication.

39. Explain media Formatters in Web API 2

Web API will handle JSON and XML formats which is based on the Accept and Content-Type header values.

The Media-Type Formatters are classes which will be responsible for serializing request/response data therefore that web API will understand the request data format and send data in the format that client expects.

Technically MediaTypeFormatter is an abstract class from which JsonMediaTypeFormatter and XmlMediaTypeFormatter classes inherit from.

JsonMediaTypeFormatter which will handle JSON and
XmlMediaTypeFormatter handles XML.

40. How to return only JSON from ASP.NET Web API Service irrespective of the Accept header value?

The following line should be included in Register() method of WebApiConfig.cs file in App_Start folder. This line of code will completely remove XmlFormatter that will force ASP.NET Web API to always return JSON irrespective of the Accept header value in the client request. Use this technique when we required our service for supporting only JSON and not XML.

With this change, irrespective of the Accept header value (application/xml or application/json), the Web API service will always going to return JSON.
config.Formatters.Remove(config.Formatters.XmlFormatter);

41. How to return JSON instead of XML from ASP.NET Web API Service when a request is made from the browser?

We can return JSON instead of XML from ASP.NET Web API Service when a request is made from the browser in following way:

1. when a request will be issued from the browser, the web API service will return JSON instead of XML.

2. When a request can be issued from a tool such as a fiddler the Accept header value will be be respected. This means if the Accept header will set to application/xml the service should return XML and if it will be set to application/json the service should return JSON.

There are 2 ways to achieve this

Approach1:

The following line should be included in Register() method of WebApiConfig.cs file in App_Start folder. This states ASP.NET Web API to use JsonFormatter when a request will be made for text/html which is the default for most browsers. The problem with this approach is that the Content-Type header of the response will be set to text/html which is misleading.

config.Formatters.JsonFormatter.SupportedMediaTypes.Add(new MediaTypeHeaderValue("text/html"));

Approach2:

The following clas should be included in WebApiConfig.cs file in App_Start folder.

Register Formatter:

Place the following line in Register() method of WebApiConfig.cs file in App_Start folder

42. Which protocol is supported by WebAPI?
WebAPI will supports only HTTP protocol.So it will be consumed by any client which can support HTTP protocol.

43. What are the Similarities between MVC and WebAPI.
Both are based on the same principle of Separation of concerns.
• Both have similar concepts such as routing,controllers and models.

44. Differences between MVC and WebAPI
MVC will be used to develop applications which have User Interface.Views in MVC can be used for developing user interface.
• WebAPI will be used to develop HTTP services.Other applications call the WebAPI methods to fetch the data.

45. Who can consume WebAPI?
Following can consumes WebAPI:
• WebAPI will be consumed by any client which can support HTTP verbs like GET,PUT,DELETE,POST.
• Since WebAPI services will not require any configuration they are very easy to consume by any client.
• Even portable devices like Mobile devices can easily consume WebAPI.It is the biggest advantages of WebAPI.

46. How are Requests mapped to Action methods in WebAPI?
Since WebAPI will use HTTP verbs so a client which can consume a WebAPI requires some way to call the WebAPI method.
Client will use HTTP verbs to call the WebAPI action methods.For example to call a method called GetEmployee a client will use a jQuery method as:

```
1 $.get("/api/Employees/1", null, function(response) {
2 $("#employees").html(response);
3 });
```

Therefore, there is no mention of the method name above.Instead GetEmployee method will be called using the GET HTTP verb.
We define the GetEmployee method as:

```
1 [HttpGet]
2 public void GetEmployee(int id)
3 {
4 StudentRepository.Get(id);
5 }
```

As we will see the GetEmployee method is decorated with the [HttpGet]

attribute.We will use different verbs to map the different HTTP requests:
• HttpGet
• HttpPost
• HttpPut
• HttpDelete

47. Can the HTTP request will be mapped to action method without using the HTTP attribute ?

There are actually two ways to map the HTTP request for action method.One of the ways is to use the attribute on the action method .There is another way is to just name method starting with the HTTP verb.For example if we required to define a GET method we can define it as:

```
1 public void GetEmployee(int id)
2 {
3 StudentRepository.Get(id);
4 }
```

The above method will be automatically mapped with the GET request since it can start with GET.

48. What is the base class of WebAPI controllers?

APIController is the base class from which all WebAPI controller derive
Providing an alias to WebAPI action method
By using the ActionName attribute.For example we Can rename the GetEmployee action method as:

```
1 [ActionName("GetSingleEmployee")]
2 public void GetEmployee(int id)
3 {
4 StudentRepository.Get(id);
5 }
```

49. What types can WebAPI action method return?

WebAPI will return any of the following types:
• **void** This means WebAPI will not returns any data.
• **HttpResponseMessage** This allows to have control over the response.
• **IHttpActionResult** This acts as the factory for creating HttpResponseMessage.
• **Custom type** Any custom type.WebAPI uses different Media formatters to serialize custom type.

50. Can a WebPI return an HTML View?

WebAPI will return data so views will not returned from WebAPI.If we want to return views then using MVC is better idea.

51. How can you give a different name to action method ?

We will provide a different name to action methof by using the ActionName attribute.For example if we want to rename a method called GetStudent to search then We can use the ActionName attribute as:

```
1 [ActionName("search")]
2 public ActionResult GetStudent(int id)
3 {
4 // get student from the database
5 return View();
6 }
```

52. What is routing in WebAPI?

Routing in WebAPI is used to match URLs with different routes.Routes specify which controller and action can handle the request.Routes will be added to the routing table in the WebApiConfig.cs as:

```
1 routes.MapHttpRoute(
2 name: "API Default",
3 routeTemplate: "api/{controller}/{id}",
4 defaults: new { id = RouteParameter.Optional }
5 );
```

Routing mechanism can also be used in MVC.

53. What is MessageHandler?

Message handler can be used to receive an HTTP request and to return HTTP response.Message handlers will be implemented as classes deriving from HttpMessageHandler.They will implement the cross-cutting concerns.

54. How WebAPI is useful in creating RESTful web services

REST is stand for 'Representational State Transfer'.It is an architectural pattern and will use HTTP as the communication meachnism.In a REST API ,resources will be the entities which are represented using different end points.

55. WebAPI is used for creating RESTful web services?

WebAPI controllers will represent different entities in application and different action methods will be mapped using HTTP verbs like POST and GET.

56. Will you lose all of your work if you accidentally exit a container?

No, We won't lose any information, data and other parameters if we accidentally exit the Docker container. The only way to lose progress would be to issue a specific command to delete the container – exiting it won't do the files within any harm.

57. Can Web API return view in MVC?

We will not return view from Web API.

58. How to restrict access to methods with specific HTTP verbs in Web API?

With the help of Attributes such as http verbs one will implement access restrictions in Web API.

We will define HTTP verbs as attribute over method for restricting access.

Example :

```
[HttpPost]
public void SampleMethod(SampleClass obj)
{
//logic
}
```

59. What is Web API Routing?

Routing is pattern matching such as in MVC.

All routes can get registered in Route Tables.

Example :

```
Routes.MapHttpRoute(
Name: "SampleWebAPIRoute",
routeTemplate: "api/{controller}/{id}
defaults: new { id = RouteParameter.Optional}
};
```

60. What are the return types supported in Web API?

A A Web API controller action will return any of the following:

1. void – this type returns will empty content (Status Code :204)

2. HttpResponseMessage – this can convert response for an HTTP response message.

3. IHttpActionResult – internally calls will ExecuteAsync for creating an HttpResponseMessage.

4. Some other type – we will write the serialized return value into the response body.

61. What is the namespace for IHttpActionResult return type in Web API?

System.Web.Http.Results namespace

62. What is the disadvantage of "Other Return Types" in Web API?

The main disadvantage of this approach is that we will not directly return an error code such as 404 error.

63. What are the default media types supported by Web API?

Web API will support XML, JSON, form-urlencoded data, BSON and also can support additional media types by writing a media formatter.

64. How do you construct HtmlResponseMessage?

Following is the way for constructing to do,

```
public class TestController : ApiController
{
public HttpResponseMessage Get()
{
HttpResponseMessage response =
Request.CreateResponse(HttpStatusCode.OK, "value");
response.Content = new StringContent("Testing", Encoding.Unicode);
response.Headers.CacheControl = new CacheControlHeaderValue()
{
MaxAge = TimeSpan.FromMinutes(20)
};
return response;
}
}
```

65. What is the status code for "Emptry return type" in Web API?

void will return empty content and its code is 204.

66. What is HTTPResponseMessage?

This will represent the response of the WebAPI action method.It can allow to return the data along with the status code such as success or failure.
In the following example if the passed Roll Number exists in the list of students then the method returns the Student object and the status code "OK" while if the roll number doesn't exists then "NotFound" status code is returned

```
1 public HttpResponseMessage GetStudent(int number)
2 {
3 Student stud = studentList.Where(student => student.rollNo
```

```
4 == number).FirstOrDefault();
5 if (stud != null)
6 {
7 return
8 Request.CreateResponse(HttpStatusCode.OK,
9 stud);
10 }
11 else
12 {
13 return Request.CreateErrorResponse(HttpStatusCode.NotFound, "Student Not Found");
}
}
```

67. Is it possible to have MVC kind of routing in Web API?
Yes, we will implement MVC kind of routing in Web API.

68. Where is the route is defined in Web API?
Route can be defined in the WebApiConfig.cs file, that will be placed in the App_Start directory.
App_Start –> WebApiConfig.cs
routes.MapHttpRoute(
name: "myroute",
routeTemplate: "api/{controller}/{id}",
defaults: new { id = RouteParameter.Optional }
);

69. Why "api/" segment is used in Web API routing?
It will be used for avoiding collisions with ASP.NET MVC routing

70. Explain Action Results in WebAPI ?
void : Nothing return
HttpResponseMessage : Convert directly to HTTp Response message
IHttpActionResult : Call ExecuteAsync for creating an HttpResponseMessage, change to an HTTP response message.
Some other type : Write a serialized return value
HttpResponseMessage Example :

```
public HttpResponseMessage GetData()
{
HttpResponseMessage response =
```

```
Request.CreateResponse(HttpStatusCode.OK, "value");
response.Content = new StringContent("hello", Encoding.Unicode);
response.Headers.CacheControl = new CacheControlHeaderValue()
{
MaxAge = TimeSpan.FromMinutes(20)
};
return response;
}


public HttpResponseMessage GetData()
{
// Get a list of Students from a database.
IEnumerable students = GetStudentsFromDB();

// Write the list to the response body.
HttpResponseMessage response =
Request.CreateResponse(HttpStatusCode.OK, students);
return response;
}
```

IHttpActionResult:

It defines an HttpResponseMessage

Simplifies unit testing your controllers.
Moves common logic to create HTTP responses to separate classes.
create the intent of the controller action clearer, to hide the low-level details of constructing the response.

```
public class MyResult : IHttpActionResult
{
string _value;
HttpRequestMessage _request;

public MyResult(string value, HttpRequestMessage request)
{
_value = value;
_request = request;
}
```

```
public Task ExecuteAsync(CancellationToken cancellationToken)
{
var response = new HttpResponseMessage()
{
Content = new StringContent(_value),
RequestMessage = _request
};
return Task.FromResult(response);
}
}


public class ValuesController : ApiController
{
public IHttpActionResult Get()
{
return new MyResult("Pass", Request);
}
}
```

71. How parmeters gets the value in WebAPI ?
The following way parameters get the values
1) URI
2) Request body
3) Custom Binding

72. How to enable Attribute routing ?
For enabling attribute routing, call MapHttpAttributeRoutes(); method in WebApi config file.

```
public static void Register(HttpConfiguration config)
{
// Web API routes
config.MapHttpAttributeRoutes();

// Other Web API configuration not shown.
}
```

73. Can we apply constraints at route level ?
Yes we will apply.
```
[Route("students/{id:int}")]
public User GetStudentById(int id) { ... }
```

```
[Route("students/{name}")]
public User GetStudentByName(string name) { ... }
```

The first route can only be selected whenever the "id" segment of the URI is an integer. Otherwise, the second route can be chosen.

74. How to mention Roles and users using Authorize attribute in Web API?

```
// Restrict by Name
[Authorize(Users="Shiva,Jai")]
public class StudentController : ApiController
{
}
// Restrict by Role
[Authorize(Roles="Administrators")]
public class StudnetController : ApiController
{
}
```

75. How to enable SSL to ASP.NET web?

To enable SSL to ASP.NET web , click project properties there we will see this option.

76. How to add certificates to website?

1. go to run type command mmc
2. click on ok
3. its opend certificate add window

77. Write a LINQ code for authenticate the user?

```
public static bool Login(string UN, string pwd)
{
StudentDBEntities students = new StudentDBEntities()
students.sudent.Any(e => e.UserName.Equals(UN) &&
e=>e.Password.Equlas(UN)) // students has more than one table
}
```

78. How to navigate other page in JQuery?

using widow.location.href = "~/homw.html";

79. Exception handling in WebAPI?

The HttpResponseException most common exception in WebAPI.

```
public Product GetStudentDetails(int rno)
{
Student studentinfo = repository.Get(rno);
if (studentinfo == null)
{
throw new HttpResponseException(HttpStatusCode.NotFound);
}
return studentinfo;
}
```

we will handle the exceptions at action method level or controller level using exception filters.

if we required to apply any filter to entire application , register the filter in WebAPI confil file

using Exception hadlers and Exception loogers aslo can handle the Exceptions

80. What is NonActionAttribute class in WebAPI?

If we required to restrict the particular actionmethod accessing from browser, we will NonAction attribute.public ActionResult

```
[NonAction]
public ActionResult Insert(){
return View();
}
```

Above method not getting access from browser

81. How parameter binding works in Web API?

Following are the rules followed by WebAPI before binding parameters –
1. If it is simple parameters such as bool,int, double etc. then value can be obtained from the URL.
2. Value is read from message body in case of complex types.

82. Can we do unit test Web API?

Web API will be unit test by using Fiddler tool.
Following is the settings to be updated in Fiddler:

Compose Tab -> Enter Request Headers -> Enter the Request Body and execute

API Stands for Application Program Interface. It is a framework that consists of various components of a small software package to interact between the applications or interfaces. Web API is an Application Program Interface used in web applications. The Web API gives lot of flexibility for the developers to build a configurable system, also it enables easy maintenance of system in future. Almost every new application uses API framework in these days.

Bibliography

In preparing this book, I have taken help from the following resources available on the internet.

https://careerkaizen.com
https://www.geeksforgeeks.org
https://www.c-sharpcorner.com
https://medium.com
https://www.guru99.com
https://www.csharpstar.com
https://www.softwaretestinghelp.com
https://www.javatpoint.com

Made in the USA
Coppell, TX
19 June 2022

79016141R00151